RAISING LA BELLE

Written and illustrated by
Mark G. Mitchell

*Consulting Editor Pam Wheat, education coordinator for the
Texas Historical Commission's "La Salle Shipwreck Project"*

EAKIN PRESS ᴇᴘ Austin, Texas

Funding was provided in part by the City of Austin under the auspices of the Austin Arts Commission, and by the Texas Commission on the Arts.

Library of Congress Cataloging-in-Publication Data

Mitchell, Mark (Mark G.)
  Raising La Belle / Mark G. Mitchell. – 1st ed.
     p.   cm.
  Includes bibliographical references and index.
  ISBN 1-57168-535-9
  1. La Salle, Robert Cavelier, sieur de, 1643–1687–Juvenile literature. 2. La Belle (Frigate)–Juvenile literature. 3. Shipwrecks–Texas–Matagorda Bay–Juvenile literature. 4. Matagorda Bay (Tex.)–Antiquities–Juvenile literature. 5. France–Colonies–Texas–History–17th century–Juvenile literature. 6. Explorers–North America–Biography–Juvenile literature. 7. Explorers–France–Biography–Juvenile literature. 8. Mississippi River Valley–Discovery and exploration–French–Juvenile literature. 9. Mexico, Gulf of–Discovery and exploration–French–Juvenile literature. [1. La Salle, Robert Cavelier, sieur de, 1643–1687. 2. La Belle (Frigate). 3. Archaeology. 4. Matagorda Bay (Tex.)–Antiquities. 5. Shipwrecks. 6. Mississippi River Valley–Discovery and exploration–French. 7. Mexico, Gulf of–Discovery and exploration–French. 8. America–Discovery and exploration–French.] I. Title.

F352.M58 2001
977'.01–dc21

CONTENTS

ONE	Matagorda Bay (1995)	1
TWO	Recovering the Ship	3
THREE	Who Was La Salle?	4
FOUR	Expedition to the Mississippi	7
FIVE	Archeologists and the *Belle* (1990s)	10
	Preparing the Headquarters	11
	Preparing the Site	11
SIX	La Salle Returns to France	13
SEVEN	Sailing to the New World	16
	Facing Challenges	17
EIGHT	Digging for the *Belle* (1990s)	19
NINE	The Karankawas	22
TEN	On Land	26
	Forting Up	27
ELEVEN	Finding the *Belle* (1990s)	30
	The Elements	31
TWELVE	La Salle Explores the Coast	34
	On the *Belle*	35
	Life at the Fort	37
THIRTEEN	Dramatic Finds (1990s)	41
FOURTEEN	La Salle and the *Belle*	51
	La Salle Returns	54

Fifteen	Uncovering Cannons (1990s)	57
Sixteen	La Salle and the Teao Indians	63
	Trouble Brews	65
Seventeen	A Tragedy	67
Eighteen	Quest for the Mississippi	71
Nineteen	Studying the Artifacts (1990s)	75
	Epilogue	79
	Timeline	83
	Glossary	85
	Tidbits	89
	Books to Enjoy	91
	On the Web	93
	Sources	95
	The *Belle* Excavation Crew, 1996–1997	99
	A Special Thanks to:	101
	Author/Illustrator	103
	Consulting Editor	103
	Index	105

ONE

MATAGORDA BAY (1995)

Two scuba divers swam through an underwater sandstorm, slowly kicking their fins. They looked for a sunken ship. But they could hardly see in the murky water.

The ship's name was *Belle,* which means "beautiful" in French. Owned by the French explorer René Robert Cavelier, Sieur de La Salle, she had wrecked in the bay in 1686.

In Texas, historic shipwrecks are state business. State marine archeologist Barto Arnold placed treasures from the morning's first dive—pieces of rotted ship's timber, a buckle, and two handfuls of lead musket balls—in a picnic cooler filled with seawater.

Arnold glanced up at the sandy land strip about 1,400 feet away. He felt good about the search team's anchorage. Documents more than three hundred years old, including a roughly drawn Spanish map, suggested this position off Matagorda Peninsula.

There was other evidence. Magnetometer readings taken the previous summer had shown strong traces of iron—a signal of something manmade under the water here. Local shrimp fishermen even marked the spot on their maps as an anonymous shipwreck.

Arnold waited for the second team of divers, Chuck Meide and Sara Keyes, to find something more. Gulls wheeled and squawked overhead, hoping it might be food.

Deep underwater, Meide groped his way along the squishy bottom until his gloved hand bumped against something metallic and hard. Two identical shapes looped up and around out of the mud. Unable to see through the dirty water, he explored with his fingers. A student of ship-wrecks, Meide recognized the handles by touch. They had been cast as leaping dolphins—a design popular with seventeenth-century navies.

Meide ran his hand down the barrel of what he now knew to be an antique cannon, until he felt its bore at the end. Just perhaps, of all the junk at the bottom of Matagorda Bay, he had located the *Belle*. He did the only thing he could think of. He yelled.

Sara Keyes, his diving companion, heard him through the water.

TWO

RECOVERING THE SHIP

The artifact discovered by Meide, recovered by a crane, tipped the scales at 794 pounds.

Technicians at a conservation lab in Corpus Christi, Texas, scraped shells and debris from the object's six-foot barrel of solid bronze. Near the breech, or rear, of the gun, they cleaned around the insignia of Louis XIV of France, the seventeenth-century ruler known as "the Sun King." Farther up, an engraved crest depicted crossed anchors and an unfurled scroll with the words *"Le Comte de Vermandois,"* meaning "The Count of Vermandois." Researchers and archeologists had to look up this name. The count turned out to be the grand admiral of the French navy in 1683, when the *Belle* was built.

Archeologists returned to the wreck, which lay just twelve feet underwater. Over the next few months, divers brought up plates, cups, and musket balls. They located what seemed to be the top edges of a wooden ship, and they tethered white buoys that formed the ship's outline on the bay surface.

THREE

Who Was La Salle?

In 1666 Robert Cavelier, Sieur de La Salle, arrived in Canada, then called "New France," at the age of twenty-three. The son of a wealthy merchant, he had just dropped out of a Jesuit seminary in his hometown of Rouen, France. His superiors there were relieved to see him go. He had too many of his own ideas to make a good priest, let alone a missionary.

A different religious order, the Sulpicians, was looking for a few good men—not to be marines, and not to be missionaries, but to clear the land and settle the wilderness around Montreal. At the time, Montreal was just a simple log village, located on an island in the St. Lawrence River. But it was Canada's second-largest "city," after Quebec.

La Salle joined the Sulpicians and threw himself into the pioneer life. He farmed, sold valuable beaver furs, and organized an entire settlement. The wilderness suited him perfectly. He felt more at home with the Indians than with his fellow Frenchmen. He loved the company of Indians because they held the secrets of survival and moving about in this breathtaking land.

La Salle did a little exploring. He thought he might look for a massive river system that he had heard about from the Seneca Iroquois. The system led to a warm ocean somewhere, the Seneca said. They called it the *Ohio*. Other tribes, like the Sioux and Algonquin, called it the *Messipi* or *Mississippi*. For 200 years, Europeans had dreamed of finding the "Passage to the Orient," a water shortcut through North America to the lucrative trade markets of China and India. Surely this massive river was the hoped-for passage.

La Salle began his quest to find the Mississippi. With some tough Sulpician missionaries and hired men in seven birchbark canoes, La Salle explored Lake Ontario. They camped with the Iroquois who lived along the lake's banks.

The missionaries, after a few weeks, broke off in search of Indians to convert. The hired woodsmen, exhausted by the relentless pace kept by La Salle, abandoned him. The expedition of twenty-four men was down to two—Robert and his Indian guide, Nika, a Shawnee who had been a prisoner of the Iroquois. La Salle had purchased him. La Salle and Nika followed what is called the Ohio River into what is now the state of Kentucky.

In 1671, after an absence of two years, La Salle returned safely to Montreal, thanks only to Nika's knowledge of the woods and the Indians. La Salle's Montreal neighbors had given him up for dead. Now, as they listened to him rave about the glories of the rivers, forests, and hills he had seen in America's heartland, they decided that he had only lost his mind.

After all, that's what happened when a person was away from civilization for too long, they said.

Undeterred, La Salle borrowed money from the Sulpicians and outfitted his next voyage. With Nika and six Canadian woodsmen, he paddled across Lakes Erie, Huron, and Michigan—bodies of fresh water as large as seas. The team's canoes glided past woods and marshes that would someday be the cities of Detroit and Chicago. But they did not locate the Mississippi River system. The Ohio River was no passage to the Orient. They decided to return home, before they had to endure another winter outdoors.

By the time of La Salle's third expedition, he owned a lucrative fur-trading post at the entrance of Lake Ontario to the St. Lawrence River, the edge of the frontier of New France.

The post was actually a fort, with cannons and barracks for soldiers, a forge (blacksmith shop), a mill, a bakery, a school, and a church. Settlers cultivated their fields and lived in cabins around the fort's stone walls. So did some friendly Indian tribes.

La Salle named it "Fort Frontenac" after his new business partner, Louis de Buade, Count of Frontenac, who happened also to be the governor of New France. The fort was the first trading stop for all beaver pelts coming out of the Great Lakes.

The pelts, rubbery and spectacularly soft to the touch, were sold at high prices to France. The fashion and garment industry used the shortest hairs for felt, which was the choice fabric for coats and hats.

The Great Lakes were home to millions of beaver. Indians knew how to catch them. An enterprising young Frenchman unafraid of dealing with "savages" in the forest could make a fortune.

La Salle was on his way to being one of New France's richest men. With some political maneuvering, he had even secured a title of nobility, a siegneury. But he was hardly content with wealth and social rank.

Two Frenchmen, Louis Joliet and the Jesuit missionary Father Jacques Marquette, had found what appeared to be the fabled Mississippi—a river so long that the two men gave up after canoeing 200 miles. La Salle wanted to follow it all the way. He had to see if it emptied into the warm ocean mentioned by the Seneca. He suspected that it did, and that the warm ocean was the Gulf of Mexico, which opened to the Atlantic Ocean.

His next exploring team included Nika, woodsmen from Fort Frontenac and Montreal, and soldiers, priests, blacksmiths, and ship carpenters from France. He recruited a French army officer, Henri de Tonty, for his second in command.

FOUR

EXPEDITION TO THE MISSISSIPPI

The expedition crossed Lake Ontario in canoes and scaled the cliffs of Niagara Falls to Lake Erie.

Setbacks included two return treks by La Salle to obtain more provisions and to straighten out problems with creditors in Montreal; a mutiny against Tonty; the loss of a ship called *The Griffin,* which they built to sail the Great Lakes; and a massacre by Iroquois on the warpath. The victims weren't French, but La Salle's new friends and hosts, the Illinois. La Salle had to start all over again to regain the trust of the Illinois and other tribes.

At last, after two years of delays, La Salle reached the Mississippi River, near the present site of St. Charles, Missouri. On a sunny February day, after a bitter winter, twenty-one white men and twenty-eight Indians (men and "squaws," or wives) shoved off through the breaking ice. The muddy Missouri River, tumbling in from the northwest, sped them on their way.

It was the happiest and most peaceful journey of La Salle's life. Nothing obstructed him but an occasional herd of bison drinking in the river. His men sang as they paddled. In the evenings, they pulled their canoes onto the banks and camped. Europeans and Indians hunted together. Indian women cooked for the Frenchmen as well as for their own families. Everyone got along.

The Ohio River, fed by melting snows, poured in from the east (at the present site of Cairo, Illinois) and pushed the group along.

The voyagers began accepting invitations from Indians to visit them in their villages. The Arkansas lived in great domed, thatched houses. They held a celebratory dance and feast for La Salle that lasted three days. La Salle reciprocated with his own ceremony. The Indians watched with un-comprehending delight as he pronounced them French subjects and claimed their village for King Louis.

Where the Red River joins the Mississippi, the water flooded out for miles in all directions, covering woods to the treetops. Land turned to swamp. Now the men fished instead of hunted for food. The most adventurous of them hauled alligators into their boats (after shooting them first, of course).

Canoes glided under towering cypress trees, the branches noisy with screeching parrots.

One day they smelled the sea. The canoes fanned out, taking three different channels through the delta.

La Salle took his canoe straight into the turquoise Gulf of Mexico. He paddled out ahead of the others until he was satisfied that the water was not only salty, but extremely deep.

Frenchmen, braves, and squaws with papooses crowded a small delta island. Two woodsmen pounded a wooden cross into the wet loam. Wearing the scarlet coat with gold threads that he reserved for important occasions, La Salle stepped forward and claimed the Mississippi River for King Louis—effective on this day of April 9, 1682.

He claimed the lands it drained.

He claimed the river's tributaries and streams.

He claimed its "peoples," "nations," "cities, towns, and villages," "harbors," "bays," "ports," "mines, minerals, fisheries"—all that he imagined the river would someday be.

With one proud swoosh of his sword, he swept 1.25 million square miles into New France.

This land today is the central United States.

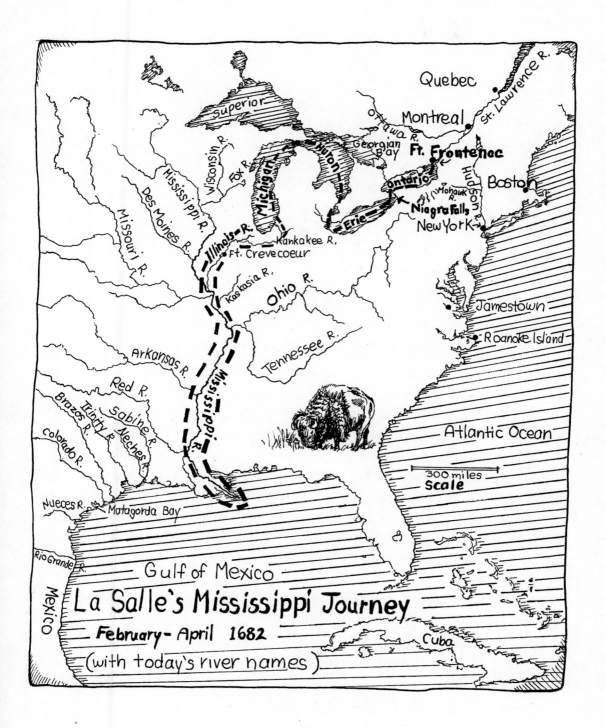

La Salle's Mississippi Journey

February – April 1682

(with today's river names)

FIVE

ARCHEOLOGISTS AND THE *BELLE* (1990S)

Archeologists arrived on the Texas coast to work on the *Belle* shipwreck site.

Layne Hedrick, a doctoral student at Texas A&M University's Nautical Archeology Program, was diving on a shipwreck in Egypt when he learned about the *Belle*.

Dr. Jim Bruseth and Mike Davis of the Texas Historical Commission had spent their careers as land archeologists, digging up prehistoric Indian villages.

Bill Pierson, a computer programmer for the State of Texas, had spent many a weekend rigging up computers and electronic gadgetry for Dr. Arnold's shipwreck hunts off the coast.

Toni Carrell, a marine archeologist with the Ships of Discovery Research Group in Corpus Christi, specialized in caravels—fifteenth-century ships she jokingly called "the SUVs [sports utility vehicles] of the Age of Discovery." (Columbus and other explorers sailed caravels to the Americas. The *Belle,* built about a hundred years later, may have owed its design to this earlier ship.)

Chuck Meide, the diver who had found the cannon, studied at Florida State University. His diving buddy Sara Keyes taught sailing at the Columbus Fleet Sail Training Program in Corpus Christi. University of

Texas anthropology student Aimee Green was back from excavating Mayan ruins in Belize. Texan Henry Thomason had just finished marine archeology graduate studies in Australia.

PREPARING THE HEADQUARTERS

The archeologists set up house in an abandoned cannery in Palacios, Texas. The crumbling old warehouse stood on the waterfront next to the fishing fleet. The crew called it "the marina," because the place also once served as a sailboat marina.

Bill Pierson brought his flatbed trailer loaded with tools from his home shop. Under his guidance, crew members put up walls and hung windows and doors, dividing the marina into rooms. They rebuilt a dock for their boat, the *Anomaly*. The new headquarters were also wired for lights, phones, and computers.

PREPARING THE SITE

The structure called a cofferdam is often used in marine construction, such as long-span bridges and offshore oil-drilling platforms. Fifteen miles out in Matagorda Bay, engineers and contractors erected a cofferdam—a fortress wall around the *Belle's* buoys. Pumps roared. When the cofferdam was completely drained of bay water, the crew would labor down inside it. They would look like they were digging clams on a wet beach. But they would be excavating a ship.

The cofferdam was not yet completely drained. But water had dropped to the level of the shallow end of a swimming pool. Crew members gazed down. Instead of an old wrecked ship, they saw thousands of frantic fish—prisoners within the cofferdam's walls.

The archeologists picked up plastic buckets and clamored down a scaffold into the steel-walled hole in the sea. For several hours in a flooded space about the size of a basketball court, they splashed around after wriggling snappers and flounders. Fish by the buckets were hauled up the wall and tossed over the side.

When only a few puddles of bay water were left on the cofferdam floor, it remained a scene of scooting crabs and flapping fish. Crew members rescued every last one.

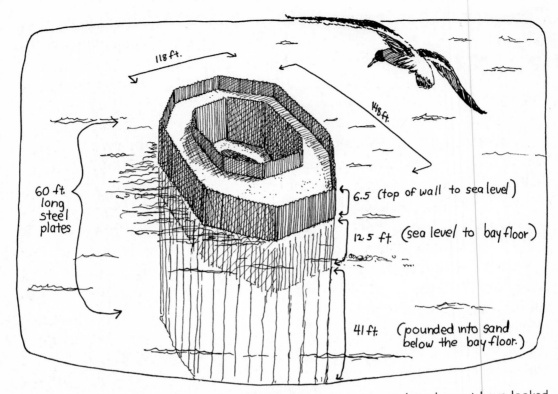

118 ft.

148 ft.

60 ft. long steel plates

6.5 (top of wall to sea level)

12.5 ft. (sea level to bay floor)

41 ft. (pounded into sand below the bay floor.)

From a seagull's point of view, the cofferdam, crowned by a gravel road, must have looked like a doughnut in the water. Eleven thousand tons of sand packed two steel-plated walls. The walls plunged forty feet into the sediment of the bay floor and rose just six and a half feet above the waves.

SIX

LA SALLE RETURNS TO FRANCE

La Salle spent most of the return voyage lying on his back in his canoe, delirious with fever. It was harder paddling up the river than coming down it. But he survived the trip, with all the members of the expedition. He left Tonty in command of their fort on a cliff over the Illinois River and returned to Canada. He sailed for France. He wanted to tell King Louis about the new land, "Louisiana," which had been claimed for him—and to secure his support for a new venture.

Nika went with La Salle to France. The Indian wore a cassock, like a priest, and a broad-brimmed red hat that La Salle had given him. He spoke French. But mainly he stayed quiet and alert, watching over La Salle like a Great Dane guarding a prince.

At the Palace of Versailles, the king listened in his study as La Salle explained his next plan. La Salle's trip had proven that the Mississippi was no route to India or China. But it did link the Great Lakes of Canada to an ocean where the water never froze. Spain claimed "ownership" of the Gulf of Mexico. By guarding the Gulf, it protected the shipments of gold and silver coming from Spanish mines in Mexico and Latin America. Non-Spanish persons caught sailing the "Spanish Sea" (as the Gulf was called on many maps) faced execution—or life in the mines, laboring alongside Indians the Spanish enslaved.

La Salle proposed building a French fort at the mouth of the Mississippi, a mile or two upstream of the Gulf. A trade center would give France a year-round, warm-water port for its fur trade—and a base in America, right under Spain's nose. (Spain and France were always fighting each other.)

To tantalize the king, La Salle emphasized his plan's strategic possibilities. With some French soldiers (his and Tonty's men), a few thousand armed Indians friendly to the French, and a few sympathetic pirates from the Caribbean, La Salle could storm northern Mexico and seize the Spanish mines. He would free the Indian slaves and enlist them in his army to fight the Spanish and "liberate" more mines. "Liberated" gold and silver bars could be sent floating up the Mississippi into New France—straight into the treasury of the king.

Tall and rawboned, La Salle stood out at court. He looked like he had come straight out of the backwoods. Weather and sun had turned his skin rough and brown as a field hand's. In polite society he seemed aloof and alone, although he had Nika with him. People in the royal circles thought him strange. He spoke Indian languages and submitted mad schemes to the king.

So they were stunned when King Louis agreed to La Salle's plan. He named La Salle commander of all French forces and Indians in America—from the Illinois country to Mexico—and assigned him four ships:

- ❦ The *Joly,* a warship with forty cannons to serve as the expedition's military escort across the Gulf.
- ❦ The *Aimable,* a merchant vessel to carry 300 tons of food and hardware for the settlement.
- ❦ The *St. François,* a small ketch, or sloop, for making water, fruit, and vegetable stops.
- ❦ The *Belle,* a *barque longue,* or small frigate with a shallow draft, to explore the Mississippi's bays and bayous.

Three vessels were government property. But the *Belle* was a personal gift from King Louis to La Salle, for all that he had done for his country.

The finest craftsmen would design and prepare the *Belle* from the best materials. She would be stylish and, as her name promised, beautiful. And she would be in hundreds of pieces! The *Belle* was designed as a ship in a kit, to be stowed away inside the other ships for the Atlantic voyage and put together once La Salle reached his destination.

At Rochefort, the navy port that outfitted ships for France's colonies around the world, the three ships were crammed with everything La Salle thought a village in the American wilderness would need.

Weapons and gunpowder topped the list. The *Aimable* also carried provisions for building and farming, such as axes, saws, garden tools, and seeds.

Altar icons, boxes of prayer books, and two sets of church furniture were stowed with cargo below deck on the *Aimable*. These left no room for the timbers, masts, sails, rigging, and other pieces of the unassembled *Belle*. So La Salle changed his mind and ordered her constructed before the voyage. She was needed to carry people and equipment, anyway.

The strong oak trees that the *Belle* was made from were harvested from a forest planted specifically for the shipbuilding industry. Many specialists labored on the *Belle* in the Rochefort shipyard, including trimmers, notchers, miterers, and bracers.

Carpenters would have used a scraping tool called an adz (shown at left) to trim pieces to make them fit just right.

No two planks ever matched up exactly, so the gaps between them were filled with caulking—a paste made of animal fat, sawdust, and lead.

SEVEN

SAILING TO THE NEW WORLD

The ships sailed with a convoy from La Rochelle on France's northern coast. La Salle rode on the battleship *Joly,* accompanied by Nika, Saget, and Father Zenobe Membre, the Recollet Franciscan priest who shared La Salle's canoe on the return trip up the Mississippi.

La Salle's older brother Jean, a Sulpician abbot, and two nephews, Colin Cavelier, about ten, and Crevel Moranger, nineteen, were along.

Henri Joutel, a boyhood friend from La Salle's hometown of Rouen, was almost like family. His father had worked as a gardener for La Salle's uncle. Joutel was La Salle's age (forty-one) and size (six feet). Retired after seventeen years in the army and looking for something to do, he had signed on as a volunteer gunner aboard the *Joly.*

Pioneers Lucien and Isabelle Talon, with their five children (Marie-Elizabeth, Marie-Madeleine, Pierre, Jean-Baptiste, and Lucien), were one of only two families on the expedition. Madame Talon was pregnant with her sixth child.

Most of the expedition consisted of men (many of them foreigners) who had been pressed into the French navy as sailors, gunners, and infantrymen.

But some unmarried women were aboard, as were a few orphans who had been under the care of the church.

Several people classified as "laborers" were beggars rounded up from the streets and cathedral steps.

The entire company, including ships' crews, numbered 280 people. They included skilled tradesmen: carpenters, coopers (barrel makers), cooks, a baker, a cobbler, a few businessmen looking for a fresh start in America, and five or six rough-and-ready priests from the Recollet Franciscan and Sulpician orders.

"It was almost like Noah's Ark, where there were animals of all sorts," wrote Henri Joutel, who kept a diary of trip.

Only La Salle, priests, and officers had real quarters for sleeping. Most everyone else lived on deck with the livestock—a nanny goat, piglets, and turkeys and chickens aflutter in pens—yet more cargo, and the weather.

"[La Salle] has covered the decks with boxes and chests of such prodigious size that neither the cannon nor the capstan can be worked," complained navy captain Tanguy le Gallois de Beaujeu in a letter to a court official.

To avoid the rain and the constant ocean spray, a passenger had to squeeze below deck and sit, bent, on a stack of barrels. But everyone was almost always damp, if not soaking wet. There was no real way to stay dry aboard ships on the Atlantic.

As for the *Belle,* her hull was designed for shallow waters instead of deep oceans, and she bounced like a cork on the waves. She was fifty-one feet long by seventeen feet wide—about twice the width of and maybe ten feet longer than a good-sized city bus. She carried about fifty people, most of them probably seasick.

FACING CHALLENGES

Midway across the ocean, Madame Talon delivered a baby boy, Robert.

As the ships entered the Caribbean Sea, pirates captured the small ketch, the *St. François.*

Days later, La Salle docked at the island colony of Saint Domingue, where French businessmen owned sugar cane plantations worked by African slaves. Today it is the country Haiti. When La Salle tried to buy fresh food for his passengers, he found that his credit was no good on the wharf. He had to borrow cash from two of his passengers, the merchant brothers Pierre and Dominique Duhaut.

Saint Domingue had a French governor. But pirates ran the waterfront. It was no place for La Salle's crews and would-be settlers. His men drank themselves senseless or died in barroom brawls. Several deserted to join pirate crews. The port was hot, dirty, and infested with rats and mosquitoes. Many passengers, including La Salle, fell sick.

When the ships set sail again in December, pirates and buccaneers from the island attached themselves like fleas. Twenty hired on as gunners aboard the *Joly*.

La Salle had to ask a pirate captain for directions on sailing into the Gulf. At last the ships rounded Cuba (owned by the Spanish) and entered the Gulf—the ocean off-limits to all but Spanish ships.

Three days after Christmas, 1684, La Salle's lookouts, high in the masts, sighted America's southern coast. La Salle did not know it, but he was not more than five days' sailing from the Mississippi Delta. He had only to turn right and sail seventy miles east along the shore.

He turned left and sailed west.

(Right) An archeologist shoots a beam of infrared laser light at a prism in the rod helds over the artifact.

The prism bounces the beam back to the total station, which reads the beam's angle and distance. This gives the artifact's position on the grid in three dimensions: horizontal, vertical, and depth.

The total station stores the data until archeologists download it into a computer.

EIGHT

DIGGING FOR THE *BELLE* (1990s)

Above and around the crew loomed a twenty-foot-high wall that kept the ocean out. The cofferdam had worked.

Actually, it seeped a little. Saltwater dribbled through rivet holes in the steel plates. Pumps siphoned away the pools forming along the bottom.

Was the *Belle* really under there?

Archeologists' shovels dug carefully into the mud.

Using the global positioning system (GPS), archeologists established the shipwreck's geographic reference point, its precise location on the surface of the earth. Crew members laid out a grid of strings, turning the bay floor into a checkerboard of one-meter squares.

They labored away in rubber boots, slickers, and safety helmets. Lying over elevated aluminum platforms called pick boards, which could be moved around the ship, they shoveled wet mud into plastic buckets.

The first finds were modest. Blue and white beads dotted the mud. A short length of rope lay exposed, one end of it knotted. A wooden cask rim and a few crates and boxes peeked out of the wet sludge of what was now archeological site 41–MG–86.

When crew members found something, they would raise a hand. Henry Thomason would photograph the object. Someone else would tag it with a number telling its grid-square number and depth in the mud. Greg Cook, up on the cofferdam road, would aim down with a surveyor's "total station." This instrument recorded the artifact's provenience, or original location, in electronic memory. The discoverer would make notes and sketches.

At the end of each day, mud-caked crew members loaded the *Anomaly* with their treasures—artifacts covered with muck and shell, submerged in buckets of seawater like live bait. On the mainland, the objects would be cleaned of rust, salt, and marine growth.

The sixteen-mile ride to Palacios, across the bay, usually took seventy-five minutes. At the marina lab, crew members washed down artifacts with hoses strung from the ceiling. But they didn't bother to wash themselves—not even for supper. They would only get dirty again.

After dinner, they returned to the lab. Small items were sealed up in water-filled, clear plastic bags and arranged on shelves. Larger items were placed in water-filled tubs and troughs.

Computers stayed busy late into the night. Layne Hedrick entered his total-station readings. The data was being used to construct a 3-D map of the ship and her contents. Toni Carrell downloaded her field notes. Bill Pierson distributed e-mail with digital photos to archeologists, naval historians, and news media around the world.

The shipwreck lay only about a mile from the Intracoastal Waterway (ICW), a channel dredged in the early twentieth century for ship traffic along the U.S. coastline.

Tugboats share the route with shrimp trawlers, freighters, and barges. Platforms with radar reflectors mark the 300-foot-wide safe passage, helping pilots stay on the "road." Otherwise, their ships would get stuck in the mud in the shallow water.

Archeologists, riding on *Anomaly*, took the ICW to work in the mornings.

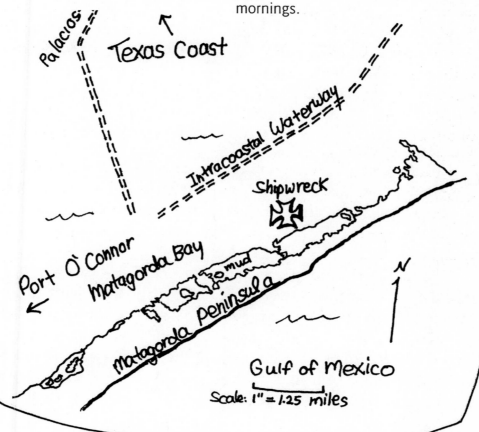

NINE

THE KARANKAWAS

La Salle paid no attention to the estuaries of smaller rivers as the ships meandered down the coast of what is now Texas. He was certain that he would recognize the great Mississippi spewing mud into the sea. But he saw nothing familiar in the numbing, endless-seeming horizon of dunes and marsh.

Tensions rose among passengers and crew. At one point, nervous crewmen aboard the *Aimable* prepared to do battle with the *Joly* as it caught up with them, mistaking her for a Spanish warship!

After arguments with his captains about where to drop anchor, and a bit of backtracking, La Salle parked the ships by a channel. A vast, sparkling expanse of inland water suggested the Mississippi. It was actually Matagorda Bay. The Mississippi lay 400 miles to the east.

The *Belle* sailed easily through the pass. Five times larger than the *Belle* and carrying most of the people and provisions, the *Aimable* rode lower in the waves. So La Salle ordered iron cannons and some of the heavy cargo

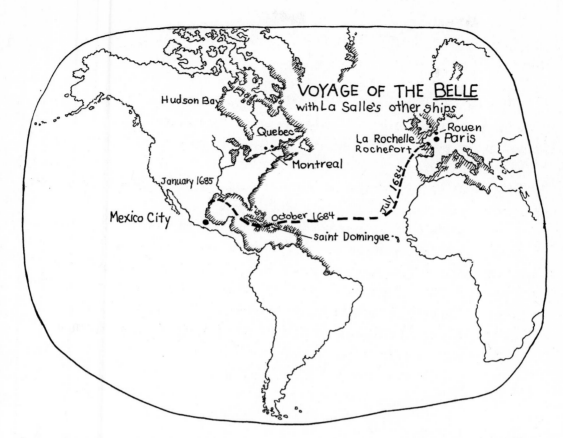

VOYAGE OF THE BELLE
with La Salle's other ships

Hudson Bay
Quebec
Montreal
January 1685
Mexico City
October 1684
saint Domingue
July 1684
La Rochelle
Rochefort
Rouen
Paris

lowered into longboats and rowed to what is now Matagorda Island. Passengers stood uncertainly on the island's wild beach. The thousands of shorebirds pecking for crabs and shellfish hardly noticed them.

The *Aimable* approached the pass, hit a sandbar, and stopped. Her hull timbers cracked as she rocked in place like a settling hen.

Father Zenobe grabbed up an axe. If the *Aimable's* billowed sails did not come down right away, the ship would break apart and sink with all the supplies. Sailors joined him in felling the main mast until rigging, lines, and canvas rained down.

For a week, the men salvaged what they could from the wreck. Then, one morning, the *Aimable* was simply gone. La Salle sent men this way and that to recover barrels and other cargo still floating all over the water.

While the French struggled to save and dry what they could, they had visitors. Karankawas—perhaps one hundred of them—lined La Salle's beach. Silent and grim, these Stone Age hunter-gatherers carried tomahawks and longbows. Their dark skin was smeared with mud and alligator grease to keep mosquitoes away. Their faces were streaked with white paint. They wore muddy animal hides. La Salle had not seen anyone like them on his Mississippi trip.

Like shoppers at a garage sale, the Karankawas began poking through the piles of rescued goods. When they departed around sunset, La Salle sent his nephew, Lieutenant Moranger, with a patrol after them. The Karankawas had helped themselves to a bundle of blankets, which Moranger was to try to recover if he could.

Moranger surprised the Indians in their hunting camp. When the Karankawas fled, his soldiers ransacked their huts. The Karankawas returned to the French camp in the dead of night and retaliated, killing two soldiers. The next morning, a surgeon pulled an arrow out of Moranger's shoulder while priests conducted services for the two dead men.

The French quickly responded to the danger. They set to work barricading the "colony" behind timbers washed up from the *Aimable*.

Captain Beaujeu announced that he was taking the *Joly* home. It was really no surprise. The plan had always been to return the warship to France once the expedition had "safely" landed. The surprise came when 120 settlers asked Beaujeu if they could join him. The captain said he had room. La Salle did not object. Perhaps his pride prevented him.

Today navigators rely on satellites to know their precise position on the earth.

In La Salle's time they used the astrolabe, which measured the angles of the sun and stars to try to determine geographical coordinates.

North Star

32° (or whatever the latitude is where you live.)

horizon

Measure the angle made by you, the horizon's edge, and the North Star. The answer, in degrees, tells your latitude on the earth.

Latitude

To find your longitude, you had to know what time it was where you were at sea, and what time it was (now) at the port you sailed from. The difference between the times told you how far east or west you had traveled around the world.

No clock in La Salle's time kept time reliably enough for such measures.

TEN

ON LAND

Men, women, and children peeked out from the dunes. Their warship escort had left. Their supply ship had sunk. Most of their food, clothes, and medicines lay at the bottom of the Gulf, along with their weapons, tools, and cookware.

The colony was a tangle of tents strung between barrels and boxes and a few cages of squawking chickens. Cannons lay useless in the sand.

With 170 people to protect, La Salle set out for the mainland on the

Belle. He had to find a place for a permanent fort. He left his friend Joutel in charge on the island.

Joutel was accustomed to living in strange lands as a soldier. He encouraged his charges to dig oysters, or hunt seabirds, or try net-fishing with him and the Franciscan Father Anastase Douay—and to quit staring at the empty sea.

Every night at sunset, the settlers took refuge behind their little fort. The Karankawas always came prowling after dark, imitating wolves. They enjoyed spooking the white intruders. The French muskets frightened them in turn.

One day, a sentry spotted sails in the Gulf. Joutel recognized the colors of a Spanish ship. He ordered men and women to crouch with their weapons behind the fort timbers. No one dared to move.

The ship peacefully passed by on its way to Mexico.

FORTING UP

La Salle anchored the *Belle* by a creek that fed the bay. He took a party of men in a small boat.

The mainland was a lonely labyrinth of reeds and saltwater pools. It was a boundless, inhuman landscape, but it offered great nesting for birds and fish. A few miles upstream, marshy lagoons gave way to prairies. Grass tall as a man's chest rose and fell with the wind, like a rolling ocean. Cacti hid from the stupendous sky under oak and mesquite umbrellas.

La Salle's men oared past a steep wall of earth. Forty feet above them, trees and saplings bunched over a dirt cliff, exposed roots hanging down. La Salle looked up. He imagined a stout log fort overlooking the drop.

Unlike trees of the North American woods, Texas trees were short and scraggly, and there were hardly enough to build the Canadian-style, multi-story edifices La Salle liked.

It would not stop him from trying, though.

La Salle brought up seventy men from the beach camp to be loggers. Cutting began in an oak grove miles away. If finding suitable timber was difficult, getting it to the new camp proved nearly impossible. Men rolled logs across miles of tall grass, pursued by clouds of hungry mosquitoes.

They pulled logs with ropes. They tried wheeling logs on wooden gun carriages from the *Belle,* but the carriages kept breaking.

The *Belle* was put to work that summer hauling tons of supplies and equipment from the island camp, which lay thirty miles away.

Overworked settlers did strange things. Thirsty men drank from brackish ponds and fell sick. A soldier ate a prickly pear without removing its bristles. His throat swelled until he strangled to death. Carting supplies up to the new site, Lucien Talon, the head of the Talon family, lost his way in the brush and disappeared. He left a widow with six children.

Loggers collapsed and died in the heat. Pneumonia and other diseases struck dozens of men. Yellow fever swept the camp, until it looked more like an outdoor hospital than a construction site. On the island, a sailor drowned. The expedition's store-master, the gentlemanly Sieur Le Gros, was bitten on the ankle by a rattlesnake. He died after his gangrenous leg was amputated.

The master carpenter, disoriented, wandered off from the job and was never seen again. Tired of waiting for him, La Salle took over as chief builder. La Salle impatiently marked the logs to show how he wanted them cut and notched. He criticized everyone around him except Nika.

Stung by his sarcastic rantings, "the men drooped visibly," Joutel wrote.

In previous years, La Salle would have stopped for weeks at a time to look for a missing man, or wait for an injured or ailing one to recover. But Texas confounded him with its deadly surprises.

La Salle bristled when Joutel made a suggestion: Timbers and planks salvaged from the *Aimable,* which the men had already cut and squared for their island fort, could be floated up the bay. It would be easier than cutting trees and hauling logs overland, Joutel pointed out.

"I don't need *advisers,*" La Salle snapped.

La Salle relented later, sending Joutel with a team to dismantle the beach stockade. The men roped the lumber into a giant raft, put up a sail, and let wind power push them up the bay.

Gradually, amazingly, the fort came together on the bluff. It was a vision of Montreal. The pitch-roofed, two-story house boasted separate rooms for La Salle, the priests, and the expedition's better-born members. A magazine on the first floor stored 100 barrels of gunpowder.

Five smaller houses made of sticks, mud, and bark sheltered the Talon family, the unmarried women and girls, and provisions that needed to stay dry. Low-status members of the expedition, such as soldiers, slept in the open or put up little tents.

Eight iron cannons guarded the compound. Cannonballs were unavailable; they had sunk on the *Aimable,* or else lay in the hold of the *Belle.* Still, the guns looked big and war-like. If Indians or Spaniards attacked, the French could always fire gunpowder and make a fearsome noise.

As fall arrived, settlers plowed fields and planted French wheat. Something like home was taking shape. La Salle named it Fort St. Louis.

ELEVEN

FINDING THE *BELLE* (1990s)

Crew members sprawled over pick boards, reaching into what had been the cargo hold. They shoveled with rubber dustpans and slurped with wet-vacs until the brown mud gave way to fine white sand. Glass bottles and ceramic jars popped into view. Swatches of brown sailcloth covered pieces of rigging rope that had once supported masts and spars. Thousands of feet of thick anchor rope lay coiled at the bow.

Waves had washed away the *Belle's* top half, including her deck. But tons of sediment had sealed away and preserved the rest of her. Bacteria that would have eaten wood, rope, leather, and cloth could not live in the anaerobic (or oxygen-free) environment.

The hull's bottom was intact—not broken up and scattered across the sea floor, as with most shipwrecks.

People called the Texas Historical Commission from France, England, Argentina, and all over Texas, offering to work on the ship for free. They included amateur archeologists, teachers, the children of a congressman, and the director of NASA's Johnson Space Center in Houston.

Only a few volunteers could be scheduled to work each day, because of the lack of space on the *Anomaly*. They gathered at the marina dock before dawn to ride out with the crew. Mainly they worked up on the cofferdam road, pouring sludge over screens and washing it down with bay water, like prospectors in a gold camp. They sifted for buttons, beads, and threads.

You never knew what you might find in a bucket of sand. Don Hyett, a commercial diver and volunteer, found a brass divider, shaped like a compass from a box of school supplies, but heavier. A seventeenth-century captain would have used it to mark off distances on a map.

THE ELEMENTS

Archeologists would look up to see the ocean rolling above their heads, waves splashing around them. They could never quite believe that they were standing on the bay floor.

Occasionally, breakers spilled over the walls and soaked the site. One morning the crew arrived to find the excavation under a foot of water, marker tags floating free. They pumped out the water and put the markers back in place.

In late September on the Texas coast, blistering heat can turn quickly into a drenching storm. The sun vanishes behind dark clouds. North winds churn the bay.

When the weather looked particularly bad, the crew locked tools and equipment away in a shed and battened down the wreck with tarps.

On fair-weather days, visitors—locals and tourists—arrived at the public dock. The Texas Parks and Wildlife ferry shuttled out classes of schoolchildren with their teachers.

Daytime callers to the cofferdam were welcome. But boats arriving after-hours posed a problem. Trespassers might loot or damage the *Belle*. So at the end of each day, one male crew member stayed behind.

No one minded taking his turn at guard duty. It meant sleeping like a baby in the portable metal house on the barge stern. The men enjoyed the isolation, the exquisite peace and privacy out in the bay, away from the noises of the marina.

One night, Layne Hedrick sat up in his bunk, trying to make sense of the sudden lurch that had awakened him. Winds had been building from the north all evening. Now rain pelted the roof of the house, and the barge pitched in an unfamiliar way.

Inside Matagorda Bay, storms have sunk ships, transformed the land above and below the water, and twice destroyed major Texas ports. In 1875 a hurricane struck Indianola, killing 900 of the town's 6,000 residents. Survivors rebuilt miles of docks, warehouses, and downtown buildings. These were smashed eleven years later by another monster Gulf storm.

Hedrick phoned Bill Pierson at the marina, waking him. "Something weird is going on here," he said. "The wind is blowing hard." Keeping the cell phone to his ear, Hedrick climbed out of bed and looked out the little window. "A mooring must have snapped. The barge feels loose."

Pierson told him to head for the cofferdam—the closest "solid ground." Hedrick stuffed a duffel bag with his clothes and camera. The bag flung over his shoulder, he dashed through the downpour across the deck. Lightning crashed.

He reached the aluminum catwalk that was the bridge to the cofferdam. The barge rolled up on a great wave. The catwalk, stretched beyond its capacity, snapped and dropped into the waves. Hedrick watched in disbelief as it sank from view.

The barge swung into the cofferdam with a colossal clang, bounced out to sea, and slammed the cofferdam again on the next wave.

Struggling to stay on his feet, Hedrick made his way back to the house. Once inside, he called Pierson to report how the barge was battering the cofferdam wall.

"Tug's coming. Hang on," Pierson advised.

Two hours later, the tug arrived. But her pilot held back, not daring to try a rescue with the barge whipping about on one mooring in the middle of a storm.

The last mooring tore loose. The barge shot free into the open bay. Now the tug gave chase and pulled alongside the deck. Her crew tossed ropes in the lightning and sheeting rain.

By sunrise, the weather had cleared. The tug towed Hedrick and his runaway vessel into Port Lavaca.

TWELVE

LA SALLE EXPLORES THE COAST

La Salle strode ahead of his troop, clearing the trail. If a danger or a problem arose, he would be the first to meet it. His men weren't physically up to cutting a path through the thicket. Most still had not recovered from the shock of landing in Texas. They could barely keep pace with him, let alone hack their way through vines and canes.

With the settlement up, La Salle felt free to explore the coast around him. He took his nephew and a force of about fifty on a march north up the bay. The restocked *Belle* followed them from the water. La Salle still hoped to walk up on the Mississippi any day.

Nika moved miles in advance of the column, scouting and hunting. Moranger, La Salle's nephew, was ordered to the rear in order to make sure no one fell behind and got lost. One of the stragglers was Pierre Duhaut, the older of the two merchant brothers who had lent La Salle funds in Saint Domingue. Weighed down with his big pack and cast-iron cooking pot, Duhaut stopped to adjust the pack and retie his shoes. The pack was unraveling, and the bison-hide shoes, dried-out and hard, cut into the skin of his feet.

Moranger, who had been last in the line, cursed him as he tramped by.

Duhaut looked up, but he could barely see for the perspiration that rolled in great drops down his face and gathered in his eyelashes. At last he finished with his shoes and straightened himself. He started forward at a clumsy jog but stopped, huffing and wheezing, uncertain of the trail. The brush around him was dense as a jungle. Moranger was gone, and Duhaut was alone.

He fired his pistol into the air to alert La Salle and waited, but no one returned his signal. So Duhaut stood frozen, unsure where to place his next step. As night fell, he imagined he saw the dreaded Karankawas lurking in every shadow.

ON THE *BELLE*

The young priest Father Chefdeville and the *Belle's* new skipper, Tessier, scanned the coast where the water gently lapped. In the distant sky, a flock of birds resembled a swarm of bees.

Only a few people remained on the *Belle* now, waiting for La Salle to return. Two parties that had left the ship had perished. The *Belle's* previous pilot, a man named Richaud, had taken his six most able seamen in a longboat to chart and sound (or test the depths of) a shallow cove. They made the mistake of camping for one night on a beach. Karankawas surprised them, killing everyone.

Two months later, five sailors rowed out toward the mainland in the *Belle's* last lifeboat to look for fresh drinking water. Plenty of wine and rum was stocked in the *Belle's* hold, but dehydration was killing the crew.

That night, the winds picked up and the waves turned choppy. A lantern was lit and hung on the mast to provide the oarsmen with a signal of the *Belle's* location in the dark. But Tessier, asleep after drinking wine, failed to notice when the lantern's candle blew out.

The lifeboat and sailors were never seen again.

So Tessier and Father Chefdeville stood on the deck, discussing their options. The question was how to get to shore. There were no more small boats. Almost no one in La Salle's day knew how to swim—sailors least of all.

They decided to try to sail the *Belle* home, back to the south bay, near the home settlement. They could wait no longer for La Salle to finish his inland surveys. They had to leave immediately before another man died of thirst.

Chefdeville, with a few others, clumsily weighed anchor. Almost as soon as they did, the *Belle* began to move on her own, bullied by a powerful north wind. Storm clouds blackened the sky. Her "crew" consisted of the priest, a teenage boy and girl, a spoiled young lieutenant named Sablonniere, the first mate Tessier, and a few inexperienced sailors and soldiers. Tessier, guzzling a bottle of wine, was no help.

Without the *Belle's* real pilot and best seamen, they could not manage her rigging or sails. The ship picked up speed in the direction away from the mainland, toward the Gulf.

Father Chefdeville and his mates dropped the anchor back over the side to try to stop her. It didn't even slow her down. For several hours, the *Belle* scudded across the bay. At last she ran aground with a sickening crunch. When the weather cleared, they saw a fragile rise of sand and grass only 1,500 feet away.

Tortured by their thirst, two sailors launched a makeshift raft that fell apart after only a minute in the waves. One man managed to reach the shore. After pulling himself to his feet on the sand, he decided that there was nothing for him to do there. He waded toward the ship—until the cold surf swallowed him up.

The survivors constructed a sturdier raft, working as if their lives depended on it—which was true. This time they would all ride, although Tessier had to be carried away from his stores of wine and brandy.

The *Belle's* occupants reached the shore safely. For two months they slept on solid ground. They lived like castaways, drinking whatever fresh water they found in pools and feasting on shellfish and gulls.

Some days they just sat quietly in the sand, keeping company with the pelicans. The only sounds around them were the rhythmic cries of seabirds and the Gulf occasionally thundering against the other side of the peninsula.

They made trips to the *Belle* to collect blankets, barrels of foodstuffs, and personal things. The raft was good for short hops to the ship, but it would never cross the immensity of the bay.

The mainland was too far away to see.

The *Belle* sank by degrees. One storm nearly knocked her on her side. Waves foamed over the deck and eventually covered everything except her masts and the elevated stern-deck, or "poop," as sailors called it. Tessier would stay up on the poop for days at a time, drinking from a brandy cask. He preferred the wreck to the dunes.

Father Chefdeville led the others in daily prayers for rescue. One day a Karankawa dugout canoe floated up. It was empty. No one hesitated. They packed what they could and gathered up Tessier from the *Belle*. Paddling with broken boards and anything flat they could find, they set out across the bay toward the settlement.

LIFE AT THE FORT

The creek below the fort attracted thousands of bison—"our daily bread," Joutel wrote. One day a wounded bison charged Father Anastase Douay, who was out hunting with Joutel. As the priest tried to run through the waist-high grass, he tripped on the hem of his cassock and toppled. Joutel pointed his musket but did not fire, afraid of hitting his friend under the animal's stomping hooves.

"Roll away!" Joutel cried.

At last Douay tumbled free, unharmed except for cuts and bruises. Joutel brought the beast down with his next shot.

With thirty-four men, women, and children to feed, Joutel encouraged the men to hunt a lot. He was in charge while La Salle was away.

No one ventured outside the settlement without a gun. They kept a constant lookout for Karankawas.

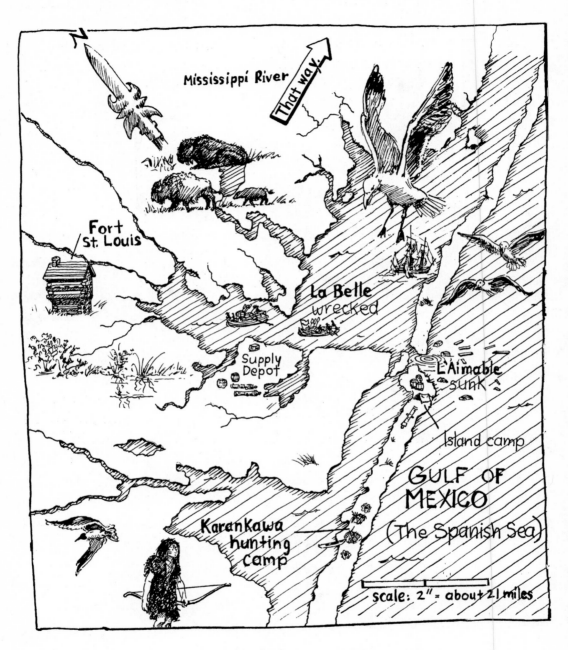

The French "Settlement" 1686

Joutel had the settlers cut away junipers and bushes that blocked the views from the main blockhouse. Everyone who could reasonably hold a musket took turns standing guard.

To hone marksmanship skills, Joutel put on tournaments. The best sharpshooters received little prizes, doled out by Joutel with great fanfare: ribbons for the women, knickknacks for the children, and swigs from the brandy bottle for the men.

One night, a sentry halted a man stumbling up the bank toward the fort.

It was a Frenchman, Pierre Duhaut, hardly recognizable in his rags and wild hair. Instead of the password, Pierre Duhaut cried out the name of his younger brother Dominique, who had remained at the fort.

The sentry held Duhaut at gunpoint and called for Joutel. La Salle had left strict orders: Anyone who returned to the fort without a letter of permission from him was to be arrested on the presumption of desertion.

Joutel studied Duhaut as he told how Moranger had abandoned him on the march and how he had managed to retrace his steps to the settlement. In the daytime, he had hidden in the reeds like a frightened rabbit. He traveled at night, when he thought the Karankawas least likely to notice him. Indeed, it was a miracle that after a month in the marshes he had survived, Duhaut exclaimed.

His ordeal seemed innocent enough. Losing one's way was not the same as running away. Joutel decided not to lock up Duhaut, one of the expedition's most worldly men. But he would keep an eye on him.

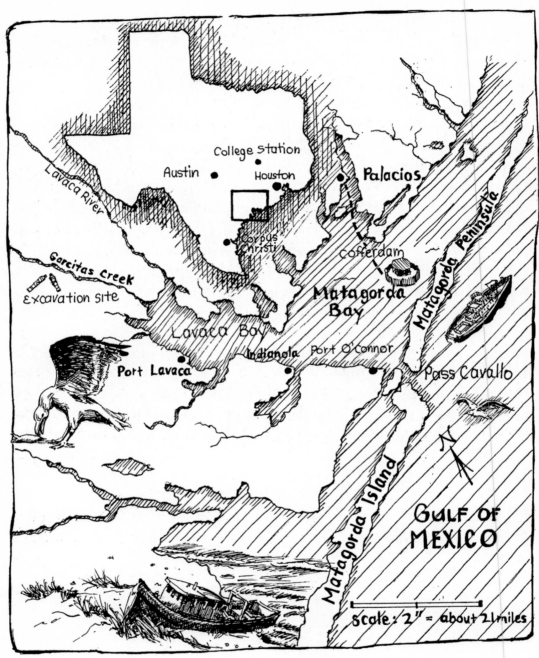

Matagorda Bay 1996

THIRTEEN

DRAMATIC FINDS (1990s)

Around the giant bay, the gulls and shorebirds are still as noisy as they were in La Salle's time. The drone of boat and barge motors is new.

The cofferdam clamored all day with noises: the roar of the generator that kept the pumps going, the whining vacs, the jackhammer bursts of air-powered chisels (as crew members banged through accumulated shells and rust), and the clatter of the lifting crane.

Dramatic finds seemed to be occurring all over the ship now. Between the two walls, or bulkheads, that divided the hull into compartments lay:

* Clothes of cotton and wool
* A high-heeled leather shoe dainty as a slipper
* A rack of deer antlers, someone's hunting trophy.

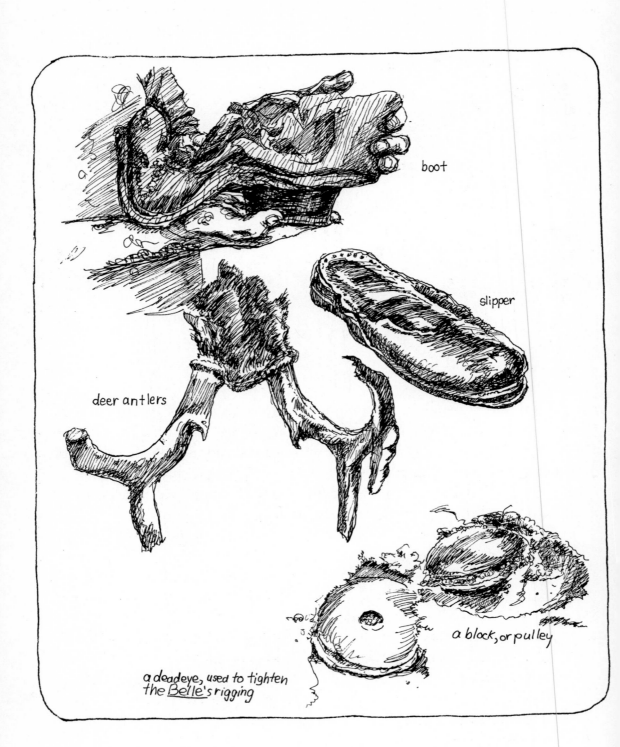

boot

slipper

deer antlers

a block, or pulley

a deadeye, used to tighten
the _Belle's_ rigging

bowl

brass candlesticks

nested colanders, pots and pans

medicine vial

cup

Some artifacts made the *Belle* seem like a quaint and cozy household:

❧ Pot hooks for hanging pots and kettles over a hearth fire
❧ Cauldrons
❧ Stoneware bowls, some with portions of a meal still in them
❧ Firebricks, for keeping food warm
❧ A wooden measuring scoop
❧ A decorative brass colander

- Porcelain plates packed in a smart wooden box
- A whiskbroom
- Brass candlesticks.

Other finds suggested that the *Belle* was prepared for war:
- Cannonballs, bullets, and firepots (ceramic bombs that held flammable kerosene and concealed grenades)
- Muskets, pistols, swords, and pikes embedded in concretions. (Resembling rock, concretions are calcium-carbonate shell homes of tiny sea organisms on the porous surface of rusting iron.)

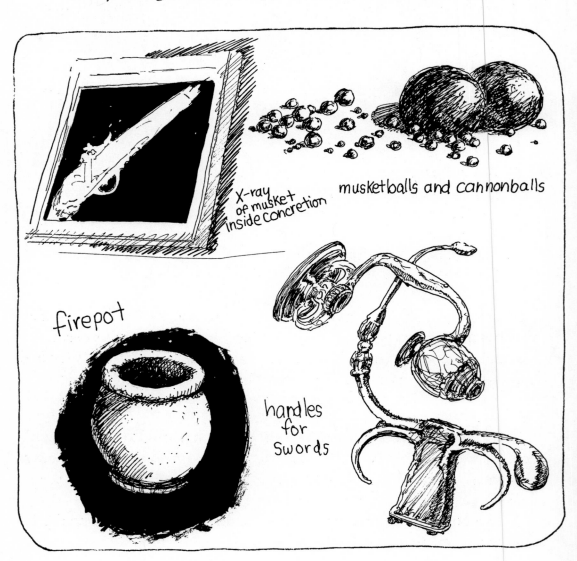

X-ray of musket inside concretion

musketballs and cannonballs

firepot

handles for swords

Crew members cleaned with soft brushes and gently scraped with wooden potter's tools and dental picks. They scribbled notes, measured, and mapped with lasers—often with the feeling that they had stepped back in time and were shaking hands with these seventeenth-century adventurers.

And there were still more discoveries:

- A wooden pulley, called a "block," tightened sail rope, referred to as "line." Another hand-carved wooden piece, a deadeye, took up slack in the ship's rigging.
- A leather pouch held two wooden combs (one to comb hair and one to pull out lice).
- There was a seal for embossing letters with wax.
- Chess and backgammon pieces were easy to recognize.
- A navigational instrument called a "nocturnal" turned up in the stern, where the captain's quarters would have been.
- A brass writing instrument with a screw top resembled a modern fountain pen.
- A small stoneware vial still held liquid mercury, used for medicine in La Salle's day.
- Archeologists often had to guess what an object was. One device with a long, sharp point suggested a giant sewing needle, perhaps for mending sails. It turned out to be a surgeon's instrument for removing bullets from men.

Archeologist-photographer Henry Thomason moved in and out of all the activity snapping pictures, trying to keep his camera lenses clean.

At the end of each day, they tucked the *Belle* in, covering all they had exposed with tarps and burlap sacks wetted down with seawater.

Layne Hedrick reached down from a pick board to the boatswain's deck. Carefully he separated the sand away from two slender black bones. It took Hedrick a moment to realize that he was staring at a human skeletal arm.

At the end, the bones of a thumb and fingers lay in a jumbled pile, along with a man's ring.

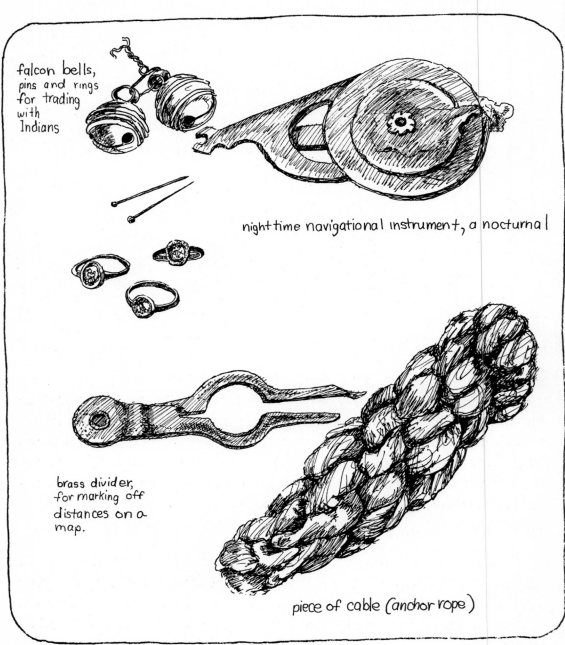

falcon bells, pins and rings for trading with Indians

night time navigational instrument, a nocturnal

brass divider, for marking off distances on a map.

piece of cable (anchor rope)

Europeans tied the falcon bells to the feet of their hunting hawks so they could identify their birds from a distance. Indians stitched them to their clothes and accessories for decoration.

A person had gone down on the *Belle*.

Crew members and volunteers gathered around in a hush. They watched Hedrick uncover a shoulder blade, a spine, a ribcage, and finally a skull.

In the weeks that followed, crowds (including television news crews from New York City and Paris) filled the cofferdam road, gawking down. Muddy archeologists, working on their bellies over the pick boards, felt like bears at the zoo.

All the public attention was good. But time was still running out for the excavation. Winter, typically hard on the Texas coast, could bring long weather delays, or shut the project down completely. The work, costing $100,000 per month, had already taken longer than anyone had expected. If they could empty the hull of all of its artifacts by Thanksgiving, the crew decided they would reward themselves with a four-day weekend.

Everyone pushed, spurred by the brisk weather and the idea of a holiday break.

But there would be no holiday break. The more they dug, the more they found. The crew spent Thanksgiving Day working at the site. Matagorda County Commissioner Leonard Lamar catered the meal (cold cuts and soda pop) from a convenience store he owned in Palacios.

Bundled against the wet chill, crew members tried to sleep on the long ride out to work each day. But not everyone could. Toni Carrell prepared work schedules on her laptop. Hedrick leafed through an English translation of Joutel's journal.

Project Director Dr. Jim Bruseth sometimes piloted the boat. Some mornings, they wended through fog so thick that they could not see the cofferdam until they nearly ran into it. A land archeologist, Bruseth worried about the dangers of the bay. What if a passenger slipped on the deck and fell overboard? Hypothermia (subnormal body temperature) would set in swiftly. What if the *Anomaly* sank in the rough waves?

One morning, the sky turned black and the winds began to howl just as the *Anomaly* docked at the cofferdam. Bruseth decided it was too dangerous to stay. Crew members, volunteers, visiting archeologists from France, and a woman reporter from *National Geographic* magazine all piled back on board. Seawater surged over the *Anomaly's* sides and onto the deck. The boat nearly foundered on her way home.

A prolonged December squall marooned Associate Project Director Mike Davis, taking a turn as night guard. For four days, no one dared to enter the bay.

Waves spilled over the steel wall, submersing the site in five feet of water. At one end of the cofferdam, waves swept away part of the screening deck and all of the equipment on it.

Davis spent the time sleeping, snug as a bug in the portable house. (It had been moved to a gravel road at the top of the cofferdam wall since the barge's retirement from archeology.)

The crew was still racing. Any day, they expected to reach the ship's bottom floor. But first they had to roll out the barrels—the favorite storage container of the seventeenth century.

The barrels lay tossed in all directions—possibly from the February day in 1686 when the *Belle* rammed the sandbar. But some were still neatly stacked. Some weighed 1,000 pounds. Many were welded together in a concrete of crud, shells, and sand. The crew struggled with crowbars, chisels, sledgehammers, and the crane.

Freeing the barrels was like playing pickup sticks, Bruseth recalled. He had to be very careful, considering each move: "Before I take the barrel that's going this way, maybe I should move out this barrel that's going that way. But I can only lift so far on this one before I have to remove this other one..."

Every crew member practiced the same care so that no precious object would be destroyed.

What had happened to the man on the *Belle,* and who was he?

The skeleton's sprawl over the anchor rope suggested that he had toppled (or been dropped) from the higher main deck. Perhaps he had died of thirst or drowned and been fished from the sea by his fellow crewmen.

For now, the man's identity is unknown.

Near the skeleton, a pewter bowl was found, inscribed with the name "C. Barange."

Researchers hope to match DNA samples from the skeleton with samples from members of a family named Barange now living in La Rochelle, France.

Computer tomography scans showed evidence of a skull fracture that had healed, and much of the brain still intact inside the skull. The scans also showed that the victim suffered from tooth decay so serious that it had eaten into the bones of his head.

A medical prosthetics firm used the scans to generate two resin copies of the skull in a process called stereolithography. A medical illustrator working in clay over one of the replicas molded a face of the sailor as he may have looked (without his facial hair).

FOURTEEN

LA SALLE AND THE *BELLE*

Joutel stood on the blockhouse roof—his favorite lookout post. On pretty days, he liked to climb up here for a look at the land.

Prairie surrounded the settlement on all horizons, interrupted by the occasional clump of oak trees. The effect was "pleasing, like planted land in France," he wrote. The oaks shaded cacti and yucca plants, while wildflowers dusted meadows with colors according to the seasons. It was March, nearing bluebonnet season.

Joutel gazed with satisfaction. Where deer and bison grazed unafraid, he imagined fat French cattle.

In the far distance, he spotted men approaching the fort. They didn't move like Indians. He shouted his delight and waved when he recognized La Salle, Nika, and the others.

The travelers carried slabs of smoked bison meat on their backs. La Salle had feared that the settlement was starving. (The truth was that it had stocked more meat than anyone could eat.)

La Salle saw Duhaut and scolded him right away. "Why aren't you in chains?" he asked. He interrogated Joutel. "Why did you receive him?"

Hearing explanations, La Salle calmed down and changed the subject. He had troubling news. The Mississippi River was not a part of this bay, apparently. And there was more, worse news. The *Belle* had disappeared. She was nowhere to be seen from shore. Perhaps rascals on board had sailed her back to Saint Domingue!

La Salle rested at the fort for a month, then headed out with his troops again. He was not gone a week when a crude dugout boat wobbled up to the creek's edge below the settlement.

Father Chefdeville, skipper Tessier, the young woman who had worked as the *Belle's* laundress, two boys, and Lieutenant Sablonniere could barely struggle out of their canoe. They had to be helped up the bluff.

Once comfortable in the main house, the six cleared up the mystery of the missing *Belle:* She was thirty miles out in the bay, stuck in a sandbar and nearly underwater.

Joutel was beside himself. If he had only known sooner, perhaps he could have done something to save the ship.

The shipwreck survivors were just glad to be wrapped in blankets and eating. "God's mercy has brought us together again," Father Chefdeville said. He led the settlers in a prayer of thanksgiving.

La Salle would be gone for months looking for the Mississippi River. In the meantime, Joutel tried to keep life at Fort St. Louis as normal as it might have been in any French village.

With so many priests in residence, every feast day and religious holiday was observed.

Joutel put men to work building a stockade of logs (such as they were) around the blockhouse, cutting the grass to control mosquitoes, and digging a storage cellar to keep all the bison meat cool.

On the long evenings, Joutel organized sing-alongs. He encouraged settlers to dance to their songs, which La Salle would never have allowed if he'd been there.

At least one romance was sparked. Lieutenant Gabriel Minime, the Sieur Barbier, sought Joutel's blessing to marry a young woman whom he was secretly seeing.

Joutel winced. He doubted that La Salle would approve the match. Barbier, an old hand of La Salle's from Canada, was from a good Quebec family. The woman, a Parisian, was poor and her parents were unknown.

Joutel hesitated, while the priests argued for marriage.

And so the colony celebrated its first wedding.

"We tried our best to banish melancholy," Joutel wrote. But the isolation of the South Texas plains was crushing. Hopeless feelings sometimes overwhelmed the settlers. They wondered: What if La Salle never returned? Did anyone besides the Karankawas even know they were here?

Duhaut told one discouraged group that they had only to say the word and he would lead them out of this accursed wilderness. No one took him up on his offer.

LA SALLE RETURNS

La Salle returned that autumn, bringing horses saddled with baskets of corn, beans, and sunflower seeds.

He had only seven of the twenty men and boys who had set off with him in April. One had fallen to a crocodile while wading across what is now called the Brazos River. Four men, including Dominique Duhaut, had just vanished in the woods, after receiving permission to turn back.

Several more had deserted to live with the Indians, specifically Indian women. La Salle had not found the river. But he had encountered a remarkable nation, the Hasinai, who resembled the Mississippi tribes La Salle got to know on his 1682 journey.

Hasinai villagers had treated the French party kindly. They had sold La Salle the horses and baskets of produce and seeds.

La Salle took hard the news of the loss of the *Belle.* The elegant little ship had been his prize, his gift from the king. She would have been their last chance to sail again to Saint Domingue, or up the coast to search for the river.

❦

Joutel walked La Salle around the settlement, pleased to show all that had been accomplished.

The livestock had expanded to an astonishing twenty hens and seventy-five pigs. There was a new chapel, and buildings and commons had been improved. Gardens burst with lettuce, celery, asparagus, and beets. Fields of cotton, pumpkins, and eight-row corn attracted rabbits and other varmints, as well as the pigs.

La Salle said he wanted the corn, beans, and sunflowers from the Hasinai planted, and fences built around all crops to keep out the animals. He inspected Joutel's meat cellar and pronounced it too small. He roughed out a design for a much larger storeroom, giving it an imposing entrance. "His plans were always on a grand scale," Joutel wrote.

La Salle grumbled about Barbier's wedding. He hated that the colony had started off with such a pairing. Not only was the new Madame Barbier from an inappropriate social class, but it seemed that a child would be born before the proper time.

Lieutenant Barbier was further complicating matters. He wanted La Salle to confer the rank of nobility on the baby should he turn out to be a boy. Granting royal title to the first male born in a new colony was a French custom.

But the widow Talon had challenged Barbier's claim. She argued that her baby, Robert Talon, was the settlement's first son, although it was true he had been born at sea. Certainly he deserved the title. He was La Salle's godson and namesake, after all.

La Salle shook his head. Oh, that he had to decide these dramas! None of it would have happened had Joutel done a better job of keeping some distance between the settlement's men and young women!

❧

At a late supper with his brother and nephews, the priests, and Joutel, La Salle said more about the Hasinai. Their society was as organized as any he knew, and their villages were large, holding perhaps 4,000 residents.

These Indians slept on real four-poster beds, raised up off the floor, just as in France. And the Hasinai grew crops and kept their large apartment houses swept and tidy.

One day, some Hasinai elders sketched for La Salle, with a coal from the fire on the back of a piece of bark, a map of their region, La Salle said. The map showed a few villages, friendly and enemy, and off to the east, a great river.

On the banks of this river lived some men like La Salle. They wore hats and coats.

La Salle paused here. He looked at his brother the Abbé Cavelier, Moranger, and Joutel—the men of the expedition who were closest to him. What if this river discussed by the Hasinai elders was the Mississippi?

If so, it was their shortcut to the Illinois country, where Tonty had his post. From here it was only a paddle upriver to the Great Lakes and New France.

From New France he could get word of his whereabouts to the king. He could assemble a rescue party, return to the settlement, and move it to the Mississippi Delta, where it belonged!

❧

The men were exhausted from the march. After a few months' rest, La Salle made ready to return to the Hasinai. Everyone's clothes were in shreds. He ordered canvas sail—the only material at the fort—cut up and sewn into trousers and tunics.

They constructed elaborate pack frames for the horses.

The priests loaded up church ornaments for the mission they planned to establish in the Hasinai village.

Soldiers packed gunpowder and bullets. La Salle appropriated trade goods from Pierre Duhaut, the surviving merchant brother. Duhaut had expected to make his fortune in the New World bartering with the natives. But La Salle needed his knives, hatchets, and glass beads, since the expedition's property had gone down on the *Belle*.

The settlers celebrated Christmas midnight Mass together. On New Year's Day, they toasted the king with cups of water, embraced each other, and said their farewells.

Then La Salle led away sixteen men and boys. Four marchers were younger than sixteen. The youngest, Madame Talon's son Pierre, was eleven. Joutel was along this time, as was Father Anastase.

Barbier, a lieutenant and the only married man in the colony, was left in command of Fort St. Louis. He would look after twenty-two people—women, small children, and the men unfit for marching. Three able priests—Chefdeville, Maxime, and Zenobe—would assist him. They had plenty of food and enough gunpowder to last them for at least a year.

FIFTEEN

UNCOVERING CANNONS (1990s)

Volunteers still picked through sand from hundreds of buckets. They emptied wet-vac canisters over screens, sifting through their contents to make sure no tiny artifact was missed. They had stayed through howling winds, freezing rains, and snow, working up on the wall, where it was coldest.

In January the crew found two bronze cannons like the one pulled out by Dr. Arnold's team in 1995. The guns' barrels lay side by side on the floor, instead of resting on wooden carriages to fire from the ship. La Salle had intended these decorated beauties for the fort he would build on the Mississippi.

The *Belle* had carried four bronze cannons, according to records in the *Archives of the Marine and Colonies of France.* The archeologists had three. Perhaps the fourth was still out there somewhere, apart from the ship. Years before, a story went, a shrimp trawler had snagged a cannon in its net assembly. When the fishermen stopped to pull up their net, the gun rolled back into the bay.

Rocks and gravel acted as ballast, additional weight
to keep the ship stable and upright in the water.

Operated by hand, the *Belle's* original elmwood pump would have acted like a soda straw, sucking up water that collected in the bottom of the ship.

Boats came from all around the bay to watch as the 800-pound cannons were lowered onto a barge for shipment to the mainland. Cameras clicked and videocams whirred.

Shrimp trawlers anchored close by. Their crews pulled up in small outboards to visit with local officials, photographers, and archeologists standing on the cofferdam wall.

Still working their way down, crew members found piles of ballast and remnants of the elmwood pump.

At last they were down to the bare floor. Now all they had to do was take apart the hull.

They chopped through wooden pegs (called treenails) to free the floorboards of the bottom deck (called ceiling planking).

Greg Cook and other archeologists taking turns on the total station surveyed each plank, before it was removed, for a computer model of the hull.

The planks were pulled away and carried to a table where they were cleaned, labeled with yellow tags, and traced on sheets of clear plastic.

They were stacked in pinewood troughs long enough to hold them. Some of the boards were thirty feet long. They would stay underwater until lab workers decided how to preserve them.

Before the crew could pry away the heavy hull timbers, they chiseled through layers of concretions and hacksawed through "iron icicles." The chemical action of saltwater had transformed iron nails and spikes into soft ferric oxide that dripped down the hull's side.

They used a hydraulic jack to spread timbers apart. For stubborn timbers, they wrapped the boards with a chain hoist suspended from the crane arm. While the crane pulled slightly, archeologists rocked the oak pieces back and forth carefully while other crew members weighed in with crowbars, wedges, and jacks.

Each freed timber was strapped, like a patient to a stretcher, to an aluminum ladder and hoisted out of the cofferdam by the crane.

Crew members guided the timbers' ascent with ropes so that they didn't flip or bang too hard against the cofferdam wall.

By April the team was down to the final piece, the keel, a single block of oak that ran under the ship's spine, the keelson, from bow to stern. The keel keeps a sailing ship from being blown sideways in the water.

It was the largest wooden piece—four feet high by fifty-three feet long—and the one that had trapped the *Belle* 311 years before. It was buried all the way in the sand and looked like it would be very difficult to remove.

Crew members improvised. Blasting the sand with water and slurping with a pump, they carved around the keel—until they could strap up the wood. The crane did the rest. Crew members could hardly believe it as they watched the long keel swing up and away, over the cofferdam wall.

For eight months they had worked together and looked out for each other under difficult and sometimes dangerous conditions. There had been no drowning or serious injury. Now they were done.

Raindrops splattered their parkas as another storm blew into the bay.

Three oak sections called futtocks were bolted to each other to form a rib. Iron spikes held the ribs to the ship's backbone, or keelson. Archeologists found the ribs marked with Roman numerals and letters—to show the order in which they lined up. The carved "B" stood for *babord* (French for "starboard"), and the T stood for *tribord* (French for "port"). A carved star indicated where the main mast inserted into the keelson. Assembly instructions from a seventeenth-century shipwright!

SIXTEEN

LA SALLE AND THE TEAO INDIANS

One hundred miles lay between La Salle's party and Fort St. Louis. For a month they had maneuvered through the mud, tall cane thickets, and dense forests, pulling their horses.

On their nightly stops, they chopped down trees and used the logs to barricade their campsite as a defense against savages.

This was before they got to know the "savages."

The inland tribes were nomads like the Karankawa, but different. They were always inviting the French over.

The Teao Indians were hosting the French. La Salle and his officers ate with tribe elders in the chief's hut. They sat on tanned bison hides and deerskins spread out on the floor.

Curious villagers filled the hut or crowded the entrance, peeking in. Outside, children played and dogs barked, and La Salle stationed guards to watch for signs of trouble. La Salle wrote the tribe's name down in his notebook. It was filled with the names of tribes learned in his Texas travels. The feat of writing always made an impression on Indians.

La Salle asked about other tribes in the region—who were friends and who were enemies to the Teao? The elders were glad to talk about their neighbors.

They "told us many things of which we understood very little," Joutel wrote.

La Salle signed to the elders with his hands, as he had learned to do with the Iroquois. "Our chief, King Louis, has instructed us to bring peace wherever we go."

He distributed presents: knives and hatchets for the elders, and glass beads for their wives. The women regarded the blue and white beads as precious jewels. The men admired the tools. They had never held steel before.

"We are only passing through here on our way to the Hasinai villages. From there we hope to go home, to our own country of New France," La Salle signed. The Teao chieftans frowned. They did not want to let him go. They were jealous that he might visit another village and ally himself and his men with a different tribe. LaSalle saw the worried looks on the elders' faces, so he added, "We will return to bring you things you need, such as more knives and hatchets and maybe sewing needles."

Wherever the French traveled, now Indians joined them as guides and helpers. They led them along the bison trails they used as roads.

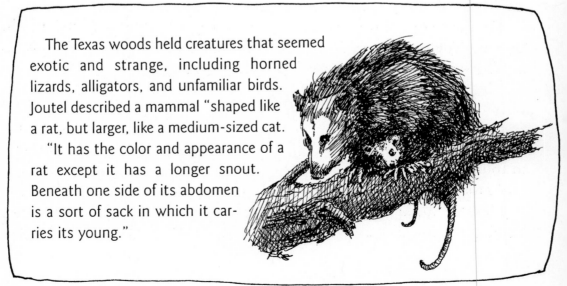

The Texas woods held creatures that seemed exotic and strange, including horned lizards, alligators, and unfamiliar birds. Joutel described a mammal "shaped like a rat, but larger, like a medium-sized cat.

"It has the color and appearance of a rat except it has a longer snout. Beneath one side of its abdomen is a sort of sack in which it carries its young."

Nika had just killed two bison. He was hard at work with Duhaut, Heims, Listot, and several others, cutting up and smoke-curing the meat over a large fire, when Moranger arrived.

La Salle had sent his nephew up to the hunters' camp with two horses. Moranger was in his usual surly mood. His job was to pack up the meat when the hunters had it ready and take it back to the main camp.

It was the back-country custom for hunters to help themselves to marrow and other perishable parts of an animal they were butchering. But Moranger didn't know this.

When he saw Pierre Duhaut setting aside a pile of bones, he blew up. He screamed at the merchant that the bones and meat should go back to the main camp to be fairly rationed out to everyone. He seized Duhaut's food.

Duhaut's face turned ashen as he stared at the young man. Moranger was the man who had stirred up the Karankawas and left him behind in the woods, and he had probably caused Duhaut's brother Dominique to perish on the last march. Moranger would ruin them all.

"I will suffer no more under this man," Duhaut vowed, his eyes filling with tears. They were tears of rage.

For once, he had listeners.

Conspirators emerged from the shadows and looked down upon the three men. Moranger, Nika, and La Salle's servant Saget slept by the fire, their turn at sentry duty over.

The surgeon, Listot, wildly swung an axe at the sleepers' heads. Duhaut, Tessier, Heims, L'Archevesque, and others stood by with pistols and clubs in case any victim tried to fight back.

❦

La Salle started out for the hunters' camp the following morning. He was concerned because Moranger had not returned. Father Anastase and an Indian guide accompanied him.

As they neared the place, he fired his pistol in the air—to signal his arrival.

He thought he saw one of the hunters, fifteen-year-old L'Archevesque, ducking low in the weeds. La Salle called to him, "Where is my nephew?"

L'Archevesque stood up. He was acting strangely. La Salle gave him a puzzled look.

From another direction, a musket fired. Duhaut popped up from the grass with his weapon.

La Salle lay dead on the ground with a wound in his head. Father Anastase looked up and spotted Duhaut. He closed his eyes, expecting to be next.

"I wish you no harm, Father. Despair made me do this," Duhaut said.

SEVENTEEN

A TRAGEDY

The conspirators stormed into the main camp, ready to pick a fight. They seized everyone's weapons and plundered La Salle's hut, then Joutel's. Joutel kept quiet as he watched them help themselves to clothes, trade goods, and ammunition.

Anyone still loyal to La Salle was in danger. Off by himself in a corner of the campsite, the Abbé Cavelier prayed on his knees. Indians in the camp noticed that Nika was missing and wondered suspiciously where he was.

Duhaut, looking ashamed and angry, ordered a stew supper served up to the men—smaller portions to La Salle's relatives and supporters. The conspirators were in charge now, he said. Life would be different. No one else would be harmed unless he made trouble.

The men who were not part of the hunting party sat around the fire glumly holding their bowls. They did not dare look at the conspirators.

The Abbé Cavelier spoke up. "In killing the Sieur de La Salle, you have killed yourselves. Without him, you have little chance of getting out of this wretched country."

The camp cringed, fearing the worst for the Abbé.

Duhaut glowered but said only, "I am sorry. It can't be helped now. It is over and done with. So let's forget it."

Then the accusations and insults began to fly. At the end of the night, when the two sides were tired of arguing, Duhaut returned the weapons. He needed everyone to take his turn at sentry duty.

For the next eleven days, they tramped through the wet winter woods—their direction still northeast. Joutel found it hard to act as if nothing had happened. He thought of La Salle and the other murdered men who had been left in the weeds. Up in the head of the line, Duhaut and the other bullies stumbled and cursed, pulling their horses through the deep mud.

Joutel wrote later, "It was irksome to be always in fear of such men, whom we could not look at without great horror."

One night when the camp was asleep, Joutel whispered to Father Anastase and the Abbé Cavelier, who were, like him, still awake, "We can kill them now—pay them back in their own coin."

The Abbé shook his head. "I have more cause for grief than you. I've lost a brother and a nephew," he said in a low voice. "But we must leave vengeance to God."

They trudged along bison paths under tall pines, until they reached the outskirts of a village.

These were the Hasinai, the Indians La Salle had said would make perfect allies for the French in America.

Duhaut sent in Listot, Heims, Tessier, and Joutel to try to buy food.

The men felt like intruders as they led horses packed with trade goods past hundreds of staring villagers. Strange black tattoos spangled the bodies of men, women, and children who otherwise looked healthy and fit. The Hasinai houses reminded Joutel of giant haystacks.

In the heart of the town, a grouping of enormous huts that Joutel guessed was the town square, young men in face paint shook tomahawks and bows. They pressed protectively around the community leaders, a committee of old men cloaked in black animal skins and bunches of feathers.

A crowd surrounded the little French patrol. Joutel, Heims, Listot, and Tessier exchanged looks. For the next several hours, the Hasinai honored them with speeches, ceremonies, and all the cornbread they could eat.

At the end of a long, bewildering day, Joutel sat dazed in a domed house where the Indians had directed them to put their baggage. He studied his lodgings—thick thatch covered lashed poles to create a wall several stories high. Neatly arranged against the base of the grass wall were wooden benches for sitting and clay pots for cooking. Splendid baskets stored a season's supply of corn, beans, and acorns on a shelf over the hut entrance.

The beds had straw pallets heaped with soft animal furs. They were raised three feet off the floor with posts, just as La Salle had described.

For the next few days, Joutel stayed out in front of his hut with crates and boxes of trinkets. He had been left alone in the village to barter for foodstuffs and horses, while the conspirators shuttled back and forth from the French camp a few miles away.

Joutel tried to be cordial to the Indians who stopped by to see him. Young men admired his firearms and traded for hatchets, or talked away the afternoons. Mothers and daughters brought cornmeal, beans, and lentils to swap for needles and pins, mirrors, and amber beads.

The village elders made themselves comfortable around Joutel's hut and rambled about battles with enemy tribes. Or that's what Joutel guessed the narratives were about. He did not understand what they said. But he nodded his head and said "Yes!" and "Good!" and "Amen!" because there was no reason to be rude.

One night Joutel stood in his hut, warming himself by the fire. Suddenly, an intruder made his way into the hut and hugged Joutel's neck as if they were old friends.

Staring at the weird tattoos on the man's face, Joutel recognized a French sailor, one who had deserted La Salle on the march the year before.

The sailor had taken a Hasinai wife and joined the tribe.

Joutel thought he could never be so trusting as the sailor. He was nervous as a cat living with the Indians. Already the elders were promising to build houses and provide wives for him and all the Frenchmen. But he doubted if he could learn their language.

The Hasinai way of life bewildered Joutel and worried him. But he had to admit that it was better than the French camp, with Duhaut and the other murderers.

The ancient Caddo Indians, the direct ancestors of the Hasinai, cultivated plants and traded with Indians from as far away as the Rocky Mountains and Central America. They built large mounds in which to bury their rulers and religious leaders.

Centuries before Europeans arrived in the New World, perhaps 200,000 Caddos lived in permanent agricultural villages in what are now the states of Texas, Oklahoma, Arkansas, and Louisiana.

Today, fewer than 2,000 live on a reservation in Binger, Oklahoma.

EIGHTEEN

QUEST FOR THE MISSISSIPPI

Duhaut announced their next course of action: They would continue looking for the Mississippi River.

Heims strongly disagreed. The trip upriver would lead only to the gallows for him, he suspected. After all, he was a foreigner, a German, and a buccaneer, not to mention an accomplice of sorts in La Salle's murder. No, he said. He would go his own way—and take his share of the booty amassed by Duhaut.

Duhaut jeered at him. The goods were his alone. He had seized them as repayment for all the money he had loaned to La Salle—money he would never see.

Heims pulled his pistol. Others did, too. In the blaze of guns that followed, Duhaut and Listot were shot and killed. Hasinai visiting the camp clapped their hands over their mouths, stunned. The French had a hard way of settling their differences!

But it was over. The ringleaders were dead. Joutel thanked God that he had listened to the Abbé Cavelier and had taken no hand in it.

Joutel and the priests and anyone who cared to join them were free to go. Heims didn't care where they went, as long as they left him alone. He even divvied up the horses and the last of the ammunition and trade goods with them. But he kept La Salle's possessions.

Several men, including most of the conspirators, chose to stay with the Indians. Like Heims, they were afraid to meet justice in New France.

But Tessier wanted to go home, and Joutel agreed to take him.

Guessing that Joutel was preparing to march, Hasinai elders encircled him. "There are no trails. You will get lost. Other tribes will cut off your heads," they warned.

Joutel considered their words. He remembered what La Salle had often said. Indians were jealous of losing their guests to other tribes.

Soon Heims was parading around the camp in La Salle's gold-braided scarlet coat, a worrisome sign. Before Heims changed his mind about letting them go, Joutel and his men packed up horses and headed into the woods.

They tramped northeast through tall pines and tangled forests. For directions, Joutel consulted his compass—and the guides from the Hasinai, Kadohadacho, and other tribes who walked with them.

After 250 miles, they stopped at a river that looked as wide as the Seine in France. On its far bank stood an odd sight—a log cabin with a chimney.

Two men in jackets emerged from a wooden door. Apparently they had seen Joutel's party across the river. One fired a musket in the air as a greeting.

Indians streamed from a village of grass huts behind the cabin and launched a fleet of canoes into the water, heading Joutel's way. They wore red body paint and feather headdresses and in some cases, bison horns fixed on their heads "so they looked more like demons than men," Joutel wrote.

The fellow who had fired the musket climbed into one of the boats. While his Indian comrades paddled, he put on his hat and stood up in the boat. "Hello!" he boomed. "I am a Frenchman, serving under Monsieur de Tonty, commandant for Monsieur de La Salle in the Illinois country. And this is the Arkansas tribe."

The year before, Henri de Tonty and a small force had canoed down the Mississippi looking for La Salle and the new settlement.

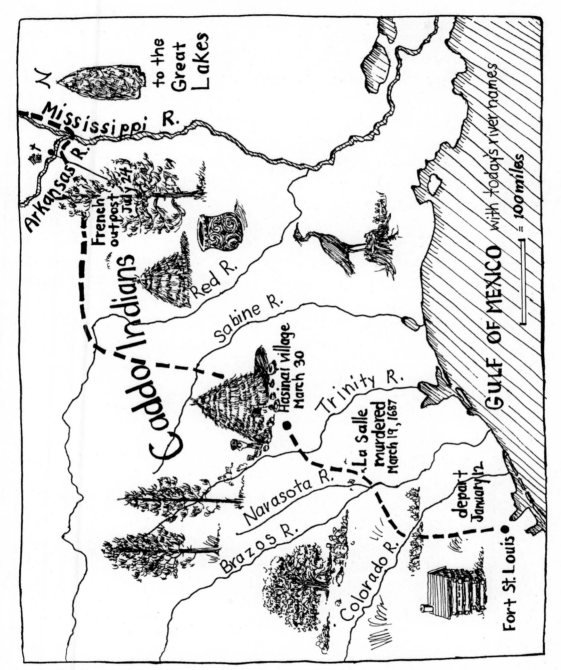

Like the Mississippi, the Sabine, Trinity, Brazos, Colorado, and Guadalupe rivers all empty into the Gulf.

He did not find his friend at the river's mouth, where he was supposed to be.

The search began. Worried for La Salle, he inquired among the villages of the Arkansas Indians, whom he and La Salle had met on their 1682 journey down the river.

The Arkansas had seen no sign of La Salle.

After a few frustrating weeks, Tonty gave up and returned to his fort in the Illinois country. He left a few men with the Arkansas to keep a lookout for any wandering Frenchmen.

This outpost was the log cabin reached by Joutel. The river flowing by it was the Arkansas, not the Mississippi. But it joined the Mississippi ten miles downstream.

❦

Joutel, Father Anastase, the Abbé Cavelier, the young Colin Cavelier, and Tessier squeezed into one dugout canoe. They paddled 600 miles up La Salle's river.

After resting with Tonty, they journeyed across the Great Lakes, to Montreal and Quebec, and caught a ship for France.

They were home in time for Christmas, 1688.

❦

That same December, Lieutenant Barbier and the priests stepped out to some of Fort St. Louis's outlying buildings to meet a party of Karankawas. Huddled in the cold, the Indians seemed to be waiting to talk to their French neighbors.

Barbier and the priests had decided to meet them halfway, to see what they wanted. It was the Christmas season, after all.

With the leaders distracted, warriors swept up the bluff behind the blockhouse and fanned out onto the commons. They left no adult standing in the yard. They entered the houses and killed settlers sick in their beds.

Karankawan women rushed the white children away, hoping to protect them from the massacre.

NINETEEN

STUDYING THE ARTIFACTS (1990S)

Semi-trailer trucks hauled the last of the hull timbers to Texas A&M University. The *Belle* lay in pieces on an abandoned airfield. Her lumber soaked in pinewood vats and steel industrial containers.

At the runway's edge stood an old wooden fire station that Dr. Donny Hamilton, director of Texas A&M University's Nautical Archeology Program, and his students used as their lab. They had the enormous task of conserving the shipwreck.

Around the firehouse, artifacts lay submerged in tubs, tanks, cattle troughs, and children's plastic wading pools.

Inside, graduate student Peter Fix snapped x-ray images of concretions with a machine donated by a local hospital. The x-rays picked up silhouettes of artifacts hidden inside the rocks.

Researchers opened barrels and poked into trade chests. Barrels held weapons, grain, and stinky black pitch (tar) for patching leaks on the ship.

Chests carried gifts for the Indians that La Salle had known he would meet in the wilderness: beads, rings, sewing needles, and brass bells that still made a charming jingle.

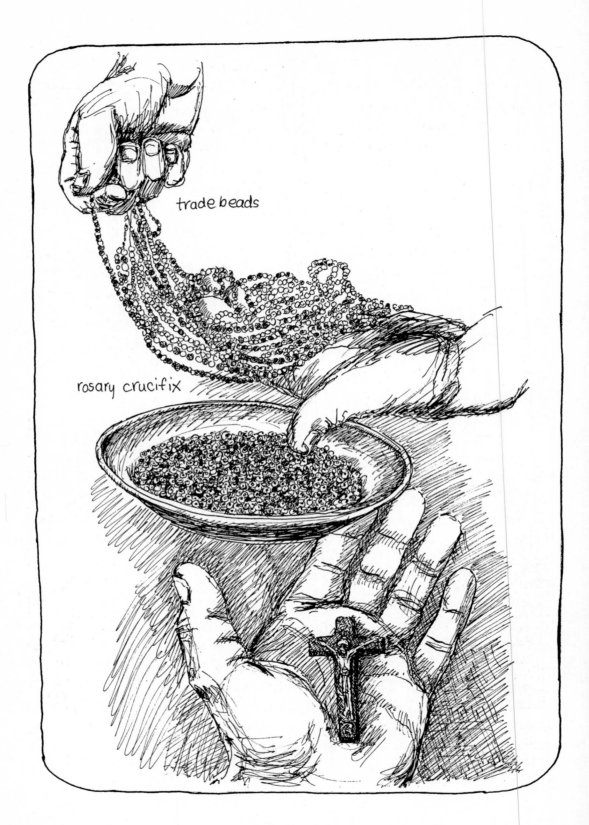

trade beads

rosary crucifix

Conservator Helen de Wolf brushed mud from a stack of pocket mirrors.

A student scrubbed a ring with baking soda until it looked like new. The faces of the rings had different images: a praying Madonna, a monk walking with a staff, a kneeling Christ, and more. La Salle's missionaries would have handed them out to the Indians as rewards for attending Mass or catechism. The Indians would have wanted to collect them all.

In the shade and quiet of the firehouse, Dr. Hamilton and his students sorted thousands of gadgets and devices from a vanished time.

When they came across an object they couldn't identify, they looked for it in the pages of *Diderot's,* an eighteenth-century dictionary full of technical illustrations. Or they flipped through art history books, poring over seventeenth-century paintings and drawings of everyday scenes.

Approximately a million artifacts (counting trade beads) were recov-

Working like old-time ship carpenters, but under water—in a pool by the firehouse dug just for the *Belle*—Peter Hitchcock, Taras Pevney, and Peter Fix reassembled the hull. The timbers had to stay wet until they soaked up the preservative polyethelene glycol, to be added later to the pool.

ered from the *Belle,* making it one of the most important shipwrecks ever discovered in North America.

Today, archeologists are still working to preserve all the artifacts. Because of their work, explorers' and colonists' struggles in the New World are being seen in a new light.

EPILOGUE

Henri de Tonty was not the only one looking for La Salle. Spanish authorities had sent out warships and infantry troops. They combed the Gulf Coast from Mexico to Florida searching for the rumored French colony.

They found it in the spring of 1689, though it was not what anyone expected. They saw a lonely dwelling on a bluff made from broken ship's timbers, and near the blockhouse stood a few huts cobbled together from sticks and bark. Several pigs foraged in an untended vegetable garden. Nobody else seemed to be home.

Their muskets drawn, armored Spanish soldiers moved into the yard, past piles of broken furniture and smashed dishes.

Two or three human skeletons provided the best evidence of the rampage that had happened only months before. One skeleton was still in a dress, an arrow sticking up from the spine.

The French trespass, pitiful as it was, angered Spain. The Spanish at last moved into Texas. Regiments and missionaries lived among the Indians that La Salle had met, and they recovered, a few at a time, the children of Fort St. Louis.

Karankawan tribes were raising four Talon children—Lucien (now age eight), Robert (six), Marie-Madeleine (fourteen), and Jean-Baptiste (about twelve)—and another twelve-year-old, Eustache Breman. Pierre Talon (fourteen) and Pierre Meunier (twenty) turned up with the Hasinai, 200 miles from the bay.

Tattoos etched the faces of all the Talon children. They were taken to

Mexico City to be raised as Spaniards. As adults, they found their ways to France, or French communities in the New World.

❧

In 1698 Father Anastase Douay, Henri Joutel's friend, the priest who had been trampled by a bison, returned to America. He was expedition chaplain for another explorer, Pierre Le Moyne d'Iberville. The venture led to the settlement of Louisiana.

❧

Tired of traveling, Joutel stayed in France. He took the job of guard at the city gates of Rouen, his and La Salle's hometown.

THE END

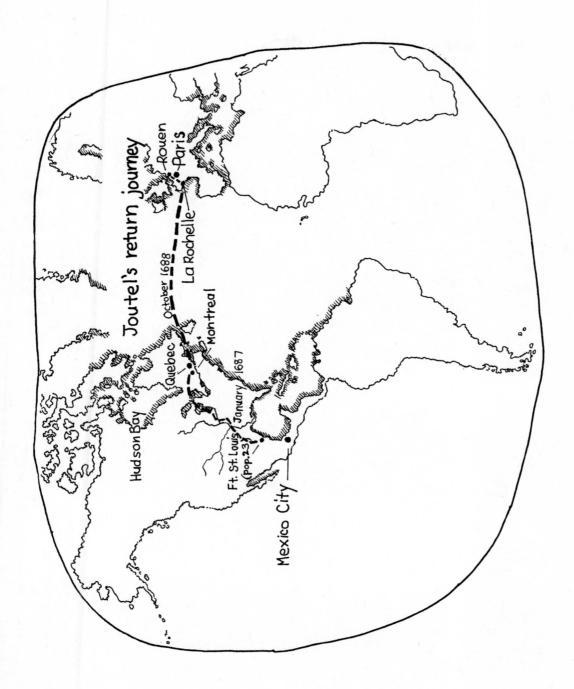

Joutel's return journey

Rouen
Paris
La Rochelle
October 1688
Quebec
Montreal
Hudson Bay
Ft. St. Louis (Pop. 23)
January 1687
Mexico City

Garcitas Creek, near settlement site.

Terrain near the settlement site.

TIMELINE

1643: Robert Cavalier, Sieur de La Salle, born in Rouen, France.

1666: La Salle leaves France for Montreal, New France (Canada).

1669: With woodsmen and missionaries, he explores Lake Ontario.

1669–71: He continues the journey, exploring the Ohio and Illinois river valleys.

1678: La Salle sets out to explore the Mississippi River and to establish forts.

1682: He reaches the mouth of this river on the Gulf of Mexico.

1683: La Salle meets with King Louis XIV to propose a French settlement at the mouth of the Mississippi.

1684: La Salle leaves France with settlers, soldiers, and four royal ships.

1685: Having missed the Mississippi River, he lands in Matagorda Bay, while his ship *L'Aimable* hits a reef and sinks.

1686: A storm drives La Salle's only remaining ship, *La Belle,* into a sandbar off Matagorda Peninsula.

1687: La Salle is killed leading his men on a march east across the land to try to find the Mississippi.

1995: Archeologists with the Texas Historical Commission locate *La Belle.*

1996–97: The Texas Historical Commission excavates the shipwreck.

Reconstructed Caddo house at Caddo Mounds State Park in Alto, Texas—very close to the village the French visited.

GLOSSARY

adz: scraping tool used by carpenters to trim pieces of wood.

Algonquin [al-GON-kwin]: any of various Native American peoples inhabiting the Ottawa River valley of Quebec and Ontario, Canada.

anaerobic [an-uh-ROH-bik]: occurring in the absence of oxygen.

anchorage: a location suitable for ships to anchor in.

Arkansas (tribe): a Native American tribe officially known as the Quapaw [KWAH-pah], who once inhabited the state of Arkansas, which was named after them.

astrolabe: a medieval instrument used to determine the altitude of the sun or other celestial bodies. The medieval era, called the Middle Ages, is often dated from A.D. 476 to 1453.

ballast: weight to provide stability for a ship in the water.

barque longue (French for "long, small boat"): small frigate with a shallow draft.

battened: fastened down, secured.

blockhouse: a two-story defensive structure.

boatswain [BO-sun]: a ship officer in charge of hull maintenance and related work.

bore: interior diameter of a tube.

bow: the forward part of a ship.

brackish: salty.

brass: an alloy consisting of copper and zinc.

breech: the part of a firearm at the rear of the bore.

bronze: an alloy of copper and tin.

buccaneer: a pirate, especially one who preyed on Spanish ships in the 1700s.

bulkheads: partition walls dividing the hull of a ship into compartments.

buoys [BOO-eez]: floating objects, often with a bell or a light, moored in water to warn of danger or mark a channel.

cacti: plural of cactus.

Caddo: Native American people found in East Texas, Arkansas, and Oklahoma.

calcium carbonate: a compound found in nature, as in ashes, bones, and shells.

capstan: the revolving cylinder on a ship's deck used to wind up the cable, or anchor rope.

caravel: a small ship of the fifteenth and sixteenth centuries.

cask: a sturdy cylindrical container for storing liquids; a barrel.

cassock: an ankle-length garment with close-fitting sleeves.

catwalk: a narrow, often elevated walkway, as on the sides of a bridge.

caulking: substance for making seams watertight.

ceiling planking: decking on a ship.

cofferdam [KAH-fur-dam]: a watertight enclosure from which water is pumped to expose the bottom of the body of water

concretions: calcium-carbonate formations, resembling rock.

conservation: careful preservation and protection of something, such as an artifact.

convoy: ships grouped for convenience and protection in moving.

cooper: a person who makes and repairs wooden barrels.

delta: a usually triangular-shaped deposit of sediment at the mouth of a river.

divider: a device for marking off distances on a map.

draft: the depth of water drawn by a loaded ship.

estuary: where an ocean tide meets a river current.

foundered: sank below the surface of the water.

forge: a workshop with a furnace where metal is heated, then shaped.

Franciscan: a member of the Roman Catholic religious order of Friars Minor founded by St. Francis of Assisi.

frigate: a fast-sailing, square-rigged warship.

futtock: one of the curved timbers that make up a rib on the lower part of a ship's hull.

gangrenous: describes body tissue that has died or decayed, due to lack of blood flow, usually following an injury or illness.

global positioning system (GPS): a modern system of navigation using satellites and metric versions of latitude and longitude.

hull: a ship's frame or body.

Illinois (tribe): a Native American people who lived south of the Great Lakes.

improvise: to make, invent, or arrange offhand.

insignia: a badge of office, rank, membership, or nationality; an emblem.

Iroquois: a Native American people of New York State region, made up of the Cayuga, Mohawk, Oneida, Onondaga, and Seneca tribes.

Jesuits: members of the Roman Catholic Society of Jesus, founded by St. Ignatius Loyola in 1534 and devoted to missionary and educational work.

Kadohadacho: a tribe of Caddo descendants, like the Hasinai, and probably the source of the name Caddo.

Karankawa: a Native American people, now extinct, who lived along the Texas Gulf Coast.

keel: a timber that extends along the center of the bottom of a ship.

keelson: a structure fastened to the keel of a ship to strengthen and stiffen the ship's frame.

ketch: a two-masted sailing vessel.

magnetometer: an instrument for measuring the intensity of the earth's magnetic field.

marooned: left to one's fate on a desolate island or shore.

moored: held in place by means of cables, anchors, or lines.

mooring: equipment for holding a ship or other vessel in place.

nocturnal (instrument): a navigational instrument, also called a "night disk." It was a star clock, which used the position of the stars to determine moon phases, length of days, time of sunrise and sunset, and even to caluculate tides.

pick boards: moveable, elevated aluminum platforms.

poop deck: an exposed partial deck on the stern superstrucure of a ship.

presidio: a fortified settlement or garrison under Spanish control.

prodigious: amazing in bulk, quantity, or degree.

prosthesis: an artificial device to replace a missing part of the body.

provenience [pro-VEEN-yenz]: origin, source.

retaliate: to get revenge for.

rivet: a metal bolt or pin.

Saint Domingue: French Haiti.

sediment: material, such as solid fragments of rock, which settles to the bottom of water and is carried to and deposited on land.

seigneury [seh-nyur-EE]: in Canada, a large estate granted by the French king, and the power and rank that went with it.

Seine [sane *or* sehn]: river in France on which the cities of Rouen and Paris are located.

seminary: an institution of training for candidates for the priesthood.

sieur [syoor]: French nobleman; "lord."

Sioux [soo]: Native American tribe, also known as the Dakota, once inhabiting the Great Plains from Minnesota to eastern Montana and from Canada to Nebraska, today mainly located in North and South Dakota.

sloop: a single-masted sailing boat.

Sulpician: a member of the order of the Society of Priests, of St. Sulpice, founded in 1642 in Paris, dedicated to the teaching of seminarians.

stern: the rear part of a ship or boat.

stockade: a defensive barrier made of strong posts or timbers driven upright side by side into the ground.

tomography: a diagnostic technique using x-ray photographs in which the shadows of structures behind and before the object under scrutiny do not show.

trawler: a sea vessel used for net fishing.

treenail: a wooden peg made of dry compressed timber so as to swell in its hole when moistened.

tributary: stream feeding a larger stream or a lake.

Versailles [vair-SI]: a suburb of Paris and the location of King Louis XIV's palace.

voyager (from French *voyageur*): a man employed by a fur company to transport goods and men to and from remote stations of Canada.

wharf: a structure built along a shore where ships can pull up to receive or unload cargo or passengers.

yucca: a variety of plant with rigid, fibrous, margined leaves on a woody base, common in Texas, the Southwest, and Mexico.

TIDBITS

❦ In La Salle's day, the Roman Catholic religious order known as the Society of Jesus, or Jesuits, sent missionaries to Asia, the New World, and other remote (for Europeans, anyway) parts of the world.

❦ La Salle's second-in-command on the Mississippi River journey, Henri de Tonty, had lost a hand in a grenade explosion during a battle. He had it replaced with an iron hand (a "prosthesis") closed into a fist. La Salle admired the way Tonty smashed his artificial fist through a table sometimes to make a point.

❦ Ammunition was precious and not to be wasted at Fort St. Louis. In the shooting contests organized by Henri Joutel, the settlers dug out their fired bullets from behind their targets to use them again.

❦ The Texas Historical Commission's official name for the *Belle* shipwreck site was 41-MG-86. By the Smithsonian Institution's trinomial system, 41 is the number asssigned to Texas, MG stands for Matagorda County, and 86 means that it was the county's eighty-sixth archeological excavation.

❦ In 1996 a ranch foreman clearing land with a bulldozer located the cannons of Fort St. Louis. Spanish troops had buried them in the clay to keep them out of enemy hands. The Spanish eventually built a presidio (a fort) and a mission over the French settlement site. So in 2000, when archeologists excavated in the brush along Garcitas Creek, they uncovered Spanish, as well as French and Karankawan, artifacts.

❦ The state name "Texas" originated from a Hasinai word of greeting: *Techas,* or *Tayshas,* which means "friend."

An iron cannon (one of eight) found at the Fort St. Louis site bathes in a trough, where an electrical current feeds electrons to it. This electrochemical process helps to preserve the corroding iron and releases hydrogen bubbles, visible in the water around the cannon's outline.

BOOKS TO ENJOY

Rene-Robert Cavelier, Sieur de La Salle, World's Great Explorers Series, by Jim Hargrove. Chicago: Children's Press, 1990.

Robert Cavelier De La Salle: A Visual Biography, by W. J. Jacobs. New York: Franklin Watts, 1975.

Ship, by David Macaulay. Boston: Houghton Mifflin, 1993.

Pirates!: Raiders of the High Seas, by Christopher Maynard. New York: DK Publishing, 1998.

Shipwreck, by Richard Platt. New York: Alfred A. Knopf, Distributed by Random House, 1972.

Indian Life in Texas, written and illustrated by Charles Shaw. Austin: State House Press, 1987.

La Salle: The Life and Times of an Explorer, by John Upton Terrell. New York: Weybright and Talley, 1968.

Everyday Life in the Seventeenth Century, by Laurence Taylor. Morristown, New Jersey: Silver Burdett Company, 1984.

One of the two bronze cannons found in the hold of the *Belle*.

ON THE WEB

Texas Historical Commission
    http://www.thc.state.tx.us

Texas Historical Commission, the La Salle Shipwreck Project
    http://www.thc.state.tx.us/lasalle/lasbelle.html

Texas A&M University, Nautical Archeology Program, Conservation
    of the *Belle*
    http://nautarch.tamu.edu

Texas Parks and Wildlife, Caddo Mounds State Park
    http://www.tpwd.state.tx.us/park/caddoan

Voyage of Doom, NOVA episode, WGBH Boston
    www.pbs.org/wgbh/nova/lasalle/

The Handbook of Texas Online, Texas State Historical Association with the
    Texas State Library
    http://www.tsha.utexas.edu/handbook/online

(Top) A piece of the *Belle* at the Nautical Archeology Institute conservation lab. (Bottom) Conservator Helen de Wolf examines the contents of a trade chest.

SOURCES

Bolton, Herbert Eugene. *The Hasinais: Southern Caddoans as Seen by the Earliest Europeans.* Norman: University of Oklahoma Press, 1987.

Joutel, Henri. *The Journal of Henri Joutel.* Compiled and edited by M. Pierre Margry.

———. *The Journal of Henri Joutel,* from *Decourvetes et etablissements des Francais dans l'oest et dans le sud l'Amerique Septentrionale (1614-1754): Memoirs et Documents,* compiled and edited by M. Pierre Margry, published in France between 1876 and 1886; translated into English by Edith Moodie and Edward K. Y. Rigg between 1907 and 1915 but unpublished. Clarence Burton Historical Collection, Detroit Public Library.

———. *The La Salle Expedition to Texas: The Journal of Henri Joutel, 1684–1687.* Edited and with an introduction by William C. Foster, translated by Johanna S. Warren. Austin: Texas State Historical Association, 1998.

Muhlstein, Anka. *La Salle: Explorer of the North American Frontier.* Translated by W. Wood. New York: Arcade Publishing, 1994.

The New Handbook of Texas. Austin: Texas State Historical Association, 1996.

Parkman, Francis. *La Salle and the Discovery of the Great West.* New York: Modern Library Press, Random House, 1999 (first published 1869).

Pertula, Timothy K. *The Caddo Nation.* Austin: University of Texas Press, 1992.

Ricklis, Robert A. *The Karankawa Indians.* Austin: University of Texas Press, 1996.

Shaw, Charles. *Indian Life in Texas.* Austin: State House Press, 1987.

Smith, Todd F. *The Caddo Indians.* College Station: Texas A&M University Press, 1995.

Sobel, Dava. *Longitude: The True Story of a Lone Genius Who Solved the Greatest Scientific Problem of His Time.* New York: Walker, 1995.

Sullivan, Jerry M., and Bob D. Skiles. *The Caddoan Mounds.* Austin: Texas Parks and Wildlife Department, 1984.

Weddle, Robert S. *The French Thorn: Rival Explorers in the Spanish Sea.* College Station: Texas A&M University Press, 1991.

————, ed. *La Salle, the Mississippi, and the Gulf: Three Primary Documents*. College Station: Texas A&M University Press, 1987.

————. *Wilderness Manhunt: The Spanish Search for La Salle*, Austin: University of Texas Press, 1973.

Periodicals

Fowler, Gene. "La Salle's Lost Ship," *Texas Highways*, November 1997.

Gilmore, Kathleen. "Treachery and Tragedy in the Texas Wilderness: The Adventures of Jean L'Archeveque in Texas (A Member of La Salle's Colony)," *Bulletin of the Texas Archeological Society*, vol. 69, 1998, p.35-46.

La Roe, Lisa Moore. "La Salle's Last Voyage," *National Geographic Magazine*, May 1997.

"The La Salle Shipwreck," *The Medallion*, magazine of the Texas Historical Comission, May 1996.

Roberts, David. "Sieur de La Salle's Fateful Landfall," *Smithsonian Magazine*, April 1997.

Todhunter, Andrew. "The Wreck of the *Belle*," *Preservation*, the magazine of the National Trust for Historic Preservation, July/August 1996.

Tunnell, Curtis. "The Cannons of Fort St. Louis," *Heritage*, 1997.

————. "A Cache of Cannons: La Salle's Colony in Texas," *Southwestern Historical Quarterly*, July 1998

Wheat, Pam. "A 'Beautiful' Historic Discovery," *Cobblestone*, October 1999.

Other References (including for illustrations)

Blunt, Anthony. *Art & Architecture in France*, Pelican History of Art, New York: Penguin, 1953.

Carr, John Lawrence. *Life in France Under Louis XIV*, London: Batsford. 1966.

Davis, Nola Montgomery. Mural depicting Prehistoric Caddo Indian life, Caddoan Mounds State Historical State Historical Park, Alto, Texas.

Dean, Andrew, and Alan Govenar. *Voyage of Doom*, television broadcast video by Documentary Arts Inc. for NOVA, WGBH, Boston Public Television

Greico, Glen. Wooden One-twelfth-scale model of the *Belle*, Institute of Nautical Archeology, Texas A&M University.

The Indians of Texas and the Plants They Used, brochure, Texas Historical Commission, Austin, 1997.

Nelson, George Stephen. Mural, Caddo Village, Texas Institute of Cultures.

Parisi, Phil, and Jim Bonar. *Discovery of the* Belle, video by Publications Department Staff, Texas Historical Commission.

Pierson, Bill. *The Cofferdam Construction*, video, Texas Historical Commission.

———. Digital photography of the *Belle* excavation, Texas Historical Commission.

Powell, Jillian. *A History of France Through Art*. Thompson Learning, 1996.

Taylor, Laurence. *Everyday Life in the Seventeenth Century*. Morristown, New Jersey: Silver Burdett Company, 1984.

Treasure in Texas: The La Salle Shipwreck, video by Educational Management Group for the Texas Historical Commission

Veercamp, Veronica, and Richard Coberly. *In Search of La Salle*, television broadcast video by Houston Public Television.

 *Funding was provided in part by the City of Austin under the auspices of the Austin Arts Commission, and by the Texas Commission on the Arts.*

Concretions from the shipwreck stay wet in a wading pool of ordinary tap water. Each one may hold an artifact.

Tubs hold disassembled timbers of the *Belle* at Texas A&M University.

THE *BELLE* EXCAVATION CREW
1996–1997

Curtis Tunnell—executive director, Texas Historical Commission
Jim Bruseth—project director
Toni Carrell—associate project director
Joe Cozzi—associate project director
Mike Davis—associate project director
Layne Hedrick—assistant project director
Bill Pierson—equipment manager, dive master, photographer
Amy Mitchell—conservator
Paul Jordan—lab manager
Darrell Culpepper—boat operator
Barto Arnold III—state marine archeologist
Steven Hoyt—state marine archeologist

(Staff archeologists)

Noreen Carrell
Stefan Claesson
Greg Cook
Gary Franklin
Toni Franklin
Aimee Green
Peter Hitchcock
David Johnson

Sara Keyes
Mason McDaniel
Chuck Meide (dive master)
Taras Pevney
Kris Taylor
Henry Thomason
    (photographer)
Karen Tier

Looking out from Port O'Connor.

Secluded inlet at Matagorda Bay.

A SPECIAL THANKS TO:

Marsha, Alice, Scott, Susie, and Will Mitchell

Glenn, Kelly, Mary, Henry (Hank), and Molly Gardner

Jan and Melissa Bradley

Pam Wheat

Publishers Ed Eakin and Virginia Messer,
editor Angela Buckley, and designer Amber Stanfield of Eakin Press

Jim Bob McMillan, Sally Baker, and Angela Smith of the
Writers' League of Texas

Dr. Jim Bruseth, Bill Pierson, and Nancy Nesbitt of the
Texas Historical Commission

Dr. Donny Hamilton of Texas A&M University

Mike Evans, writer and librarian

John Gibson, archivist, and Janet Nelson, librarian, of the
Burton Historical Collection, Detroit Public Library

The City of Austin, Texas, and the Austin Arts Commission

The Texas Commission on the Arts

**For their interviews and other gracious help the author also thanks,
in alphabetical order:**

Barto Arnold, director of maritime archeology, Nautical Archeology Program,
Texas A&M University, College Station, Texas

Sandi Brumaster, Don's Diving Service, Palacios, Texas

Dr. Jim Bruseth, director, La Salle Shipwreck Project, and the Division of
Archeology, Texas Historical Commission, Austin, Texas

Toni Carrell, assistant project director, La Salle Shipwreck Project, Ships of Exploration and Discovery Research, Corpus Christi, Texas

Colleen Claybourn, historian, Palacios

Mike Davis, director, Fort St. Louis Excavation; associate director, La Salle Shipwreck Project, Texas Historical Commission, Austin

Helen Dewolf, Conservation Lab, Nautical Archeology Program, Texas A&M University, College Station

Oliver Franklin, Republic of Texas Museum, Texas Historical Association, Austin

Dr. Donny Hamilton, program director, Conservation Research Laboratory, Nautical Archeology Program, Department of Anthropology, Texas A&M University College of Liberal Arts, College Station

Billy and Dollie Hamlin, managers, Luther Hotel, Palacios

Joyce Harvey, Texas State Marine Education Center, Palacios

Layne Hedrick, assistant project director, La Salle Shipwreck Project, Texas Historical Commission, Austin

Jim Herold, site manager, Caddoan Mounds State Historical Park, Alto, Texas

Peter Hitchcock, La Salle Shipwreck Project crew, staff archeologist, THC, Conservation Lab, Nautical Archeology Program, Texas A&M University, College Station

Dr. Steven D. Hoyt, state marine archeologist, Texas Historical Commission, Austin

Captain Donald G. Hyett, commercial diver, scuba instructor, dive master for La Salle Shipwreck Project; owner, Don's Diving Service, Palacios

Ed Johnson, Institute of Texan Cultures, San Antonio, Texas

Leonard Lamar, commissioner Precinct 3, Matagorda County, Palacios

Bob Miller, Miller Blueprint, Austin (supplier of the excavation's total-station surveying technology)

Bill Pierson, manager of operations, dive master, La Salle Shipwreck Project; Fort St. Louis Excavation, Texas Historical Commission, Austin

Dale Porter, ACE Hardware Store, Palacios

Gail Purvis, director, The Trull Foundation, Palacios

Henry Thomason, marine archeologist, photographer, crew member, La Salle Shipwreck Project; archeologist, Texas Historical Commission, Austin

Erik Tschanz, park manager, Matagorda Island State Park, Texas Parks & Wildlife, Port O'Connor, Texas

Pam Wheat, Houston

AUTHOR/ILLUSTRATOR

Mark G. Mitchell has created two other books for Eakin Press, *The Mustang Professor* and *Seeing Stars: McDonald Observatory, Its Science and Astronomers*.

His illustrations also have appeared in several books by other authors, as well the children's history magazines *Cobblestone* and *AppleSeeds*.

He lives in Austin with his wife, Marsha.

CONSULTING EDITOR

Pam Wheat is the executive director of the Texas Archeological Society and the past director of education at the Houston Museum of Natural Science.

An educator, archeologist, and former president of the Texas Archeological Society, she served the Texas Historical Commission as the education coordinator for the La Salle Shipwreck Project during the excavation.

She holds an MA in history from the University of Texas at Austin.

Statue of La Salle, located at Indianola.

INDEX

adz, 15
Aimable (ship), 14, 22, 23, 24
Algonquin Indians, 5
Anastase, Father, 56, 65–66, 68, 74
Anomaly (ship) 11, 20, 21, 30, 48–49
Archives of the Marine and Colonies of France, 57
Arkansas Indians, 8, 72, 74
Arkansas River, 74
Arnold, Barto, 1–2, 10, 57
astrolabe, 25
Atlantic Ocean, 6
Barange, C., 50
Barbier, Lieutenant, 54–55, 74
barque longue, 14
Beaujeu, Tanguy le Gallois de, 17, 24
beaver, 6
Belle, the: artifacts from, 3, 19–20, 31, 41–47, 49, 57, 75; design of, 15; discovery of, 1–2; excavation of, 19–21, 30–31, 41–49, 59–61; and Fort St. Louis, 26–27, 28; as gift, 14–15; pulling out keel of, 60–61; recovery of, 3; sailing, 23; shipwreck site, 10–12; sinking of, 36–37; skeleton from, 45–47, 50; wreck of, 35–36
Binger, Oklahoma, 70
bison, 37, 51, 52, 65
Brazos River, 54
Breman, Eustache, 79

Bruseth, Jim, 10, 48, 49
Buade, Louis de, 6
Caddo Indians, 70
Cairo, Illinois, 8
caravels, 10
Caribbean Sea, 17
Carrell, Toni, 10, 20, 48
caulking, 15
Cavelier, Abbé, 55, 67–68, 71, 74
Cavelier, Colin, 16, 74
Cavelier, Jean, 16
Cavelier, René Robert. *See* La Salle
Chefdeville, Father, 35–36, 37, 52, 56
cofferdam, 11–12, 19, 32
Colorado River, 73
Cook, Greg, 20, 60
Cuba, 18
d'Iberville, Pierre Le Moyne, 80
Davis, Mike, 10, 49
de Wolf, Helen, 77, 94
Diderot's (dictionary), 77
Douay, Anastase, 27, 37, 80
Duhaut, Dominique, 18, 39, 54, 65
Duhaut, Pierre, 18, 34–35, 39, 52, 53, 56, 65–66, 67–68, 69, 71
Fix, Peter, 75, 77
Fort Frontenac, 5–6
Fort St. Louis: and disease, 28; farming at, 29; housing at, 28–29; life at, 37,

39, 52-53; and logging, 27-28; massacre at, 74; and overwork at, 28

frigate, 14

global positioning system (GPS), 19

gold, 14

Great Lakes, 5-6, 7, 13, 55, 74

Green, Aimee, 11

Griffin (ship), 7

Guadalupe River, 73

Gulf of Mexico, 6, 8, 14, 18

Hamilton, Donny, 75, 77

Hasinai Indians, 54, 55-56, 68-69, 71, 72

Hedrick, Layne, 10, 20, 31-33, 45, 47

Heims, 65, 68, 71-72

Hitchcock, Peter, 77

Hyett, Don, 31

Illinois Indians, 7

Indianola, 32

Intracoastal Waterway (ICW), 21

Johnson Space Center, 30

Joliet, Louis, 6

Joly (ship), 14, 16, 18, 22, 24

Joutel, Henri, 16, 17, 27, 37-38, 39, 48, 51-53, 54, 55, 55, 67, 68-69, 71-72, 74, 80

Kadohadacho Indians, 72

Karankawa Indians, 24, 27, 35, 37, 63, 53, 74

Kentucky, 5

ketch, 14

Keyes, Sara, 2, 10

L'Archevesque, 65-66

La Rochelle, France, 16, 50

La Salle: in Canada, 4-6; death of, 65, 66; described, 4, 14; and Fort St. Louis, 26-29; in France, 13-15; and Indians, 4, 5, 7-8; on Magagorda Island, 23-24; and Mississippi exploration, 5, 7-9; and New World, expedition to, 16-18; and Texas coast, 34-35; and trade, 6

Lake Erie, 5, 7

Lake Huron, 5

Lake Michigan, 5

Lake Ontario, 5, 7

Lamar, Leonard, 48

latitude, finding, 25

Le Gros, Sieur, 28

Listot (surgeon), 65, 68, 71

logging, 27-28

longitude, finding, 25

Louis XIV, 3, 8, 13-15

Louisiana, 8, 13

magnetometer readings, 1

Marquette, Jacques, 6

Matagorda Bay, 1-2, 11, 12, 22 , 32, 100

Matagorda Island, 23-24

Matagorda Peninsula, 1

Maxime, Father, 56

Meide, Chuck, 2, 3, 10

Membre, Zenobe, 16, 23, 56

Meunier, Pierre, 80

Minime, Gabriel, 53

Mississippi Delta, 18, 55

Mississippi River, 5, 7-9, 13-14, 22, 52, 55, 71, 72-74

Missouri River, 7

Montreal, Canada, 4

Moranger, Crevel, 16, 24, 34-35, 39, 55, 65

Niagara Falls, 7

Nika (Indian guide), 5, 6, 13, 14, 16, 34, 52, 65, 67

North Star, 25

Ohio River, 5, 8

Palace of Versailles, 13

Palacios, Texas, 11, 20, 48

Pevney, Taras, 77

Pierson, Bill, 10, 11, 32-33

pirates, 18

Port Lavaca, 33

Recollet Franciscans, 17

Red River, 8

Richaud (pilot) 35

Rochefort, France, 15

Rouen, France, 4, 16, 80

Sabine River, 73

Sablonniere, Lieutenant, 36, 52

Saget (servant), 16, 65

Saint Domingue (Haiti), 17-18, 34, 52, 54

Seneca Iroquois Indians, 4-5, 6

Ships of Discovery Research Group, Corpus Christi, 10
silver, 14
Sioux Indians, 5
sloop, 14
Spain, 14
Spanish ships, 27
St. Charles, Missouri, 7
St. François (ship), 14, 17
St. Lawrence River, 4, 5
stereolithography, 50
Sulpicians, 4, 5, 17
Talon, Elizabeth, 16
Talon, Isabelle, 16, 17, 55
Talon, Jean-Baptiste, 16, 79
Talon, Lucien, 16, 28, 79

Talon, Marie-Madeleine, 16, 79
Talon, Pierre, 16, 56, 79-80
Talon, Robert, 17, 55, 79
Teao Indians, 63-64
Tessier (skipper), 35-37, 68, 52, 74
Texas A&M University, 75, 98
Texas A&M University's Nautical Archeology Program, 10, 75
Texas Historical Commission, 10, 30
Thomason, Henry, 11, 20, 45
Tonty, Henri de, 6, 7, 13-14, 55, 72, 74, 79
total station, 18,19, 20
Trinity River, 73
Vermandois, Count of, 3
Zenobe, Father, 16, 23, 56